THE
TA☯
OF
WEALTH
AND
PROSPERITY

Block out the noise and find
your financial centre

ALEX GALVIN

R^ethink

First published in Great Britain in 2021 by Rethink Press
(www.rethinkpress.com)

Cover image © Shutterstock | beta757

Contents

Introduction

Assume for a moment that money is no object. Tell me, what does your ideal life look like to you? Are you safe, healthy and happy? Are you living with conviction and achieving your goals? Are you perpetually moving forward without limitation and with the freedom to do what you want, when you want? Are you living with purpose, love and passion, anywhere in the world you like?

Chances are your ideal life will be underpinned by your values, whether they be freedom, safety, generosity, health or happiness. But how often do our financial plans truly align with our values and vision for an ideal life? Money is a medium of exchange and store of value, the key word being 'value'. Like our personal values, our money and net worth are directly linked to our core views and philosophies in life.

As a financial advisor, I've seen money and wealth act as an enabler for all kinds of clients. And I know that the more money you have, the greater your power to connect, which amplifies your personality. If you're driven by ego, with more money, you're going to act out of ego even more. If you're kind and generous, with more money, you can spread and share your beneficial influence.

Your impact is underpinned by your values; if you have good values, such as kindness, integrity and accountability, they will influence the way you direct your impact. Bad values tend to be reactive and emotional, motivated by thoughts like 'I'm going to sabotage everyone around me just because I'm upset' (passive-aggression), 'I'll have extravagant spending sprees just because I can' (hedonism) or 'I'll name-drop to prove my worth' (seeking external validation). All these things can lead you further away from your ideal life, rather than closer to it.

During my time in financial services, I have worked for a bank, corporates and boutique practices as an advisor and an associate to a senior partner. I have helped people protect their loved ones and insure against a worst-case scenario. I have helped people transition from operating their business to retiring on their own terms, complete with dream holidays. I have helped people minimise their tax and structure their assets not just to get rich, but to have more space in their lives, creating quality time with their family and building capital that will last them well and truly into their golden years. But in all of these scenarios, I have worked to ensure that my advice aligns with my clients' core ideals and their financial gains amplify their true values.

I remember the interview for my first position: my prospective employer asked me why I wanted to become a financial advisor. I couldn't really answer the question in elaborate terms; I simply explained that I enjoy seeing people realise their potential and helping them live their lives on their own terms. I wanted to serve others and make a worthwhile impact.

I now have my own practice on Sydney's Northern Beaches and specialise in providing advice to small business owners, ensuring that my clients' financial plans are in harmony with their core values. Taoism is a Chinese philosophy based upon two opposing but complementary forces called *yin* and *yang*. We see similar dualities throughout humankind, including in financial planning, which I believe requires us to create balance and understanding between the present benefits and future possibilities of money. In other words, I specialise in the *Tao of Wealth and Prosperity*.

Another way to think about the *Tao of Wealth* is to use the concept of 'True North'. When we're charting a course at sea, there is a distinction between the earth's magnetic north and the north point of a map. A navigator must account for this misdirection through changing conditions and still manage to find a way to his or her chosen destination.

The same principle applies to financial planning. The world is naturally uncertain and life as we know it is in a constant state of flux. We must manage and control risk and keep our chosen goals in focus. To achieve financial success as well as personal fulfilment, we must not blindly follow the herd; we must navigate according to our own True North.

This book is for anyone who wants their personal finances to serve them rather than the other way around. It's for people that want to grow their wealth, but who know that real happiness lies not in the size of a bank account, but in spending time with the people they love and pursuing meaningful goals. These are the kind of people who know the value of community and family and don't want to squander their energy fixating on things that don't bring them joy.

Unfortunately, it is these people who can become lost in the financial woods. Like Alice in Wonderland receiving advice 'looking through the glass' from Mad Hatters and untrustworthy Cheshire Cats, they follow the herd into terrible investments or are talked into a superannuation scheme that's just not the right fit for their stage in life. They find themselves in a hamster wheel, trying to stick to a budget that's actually costing them money, or placing their money into investments that require more time, energy and specialist knowledge than they have to give. All too often, they are burned by big losses or simply give up because things are too complicated. They rush into defensive investments, which is like hiding money under the bed, or leave their savings in dead-end assets for decades. And by doing this, they lose thousands of dollars, sometimes hundreds of thousands of dollars, that might have gone towards funding a comfortable retirement.

The truth is that managing your personal finances should not be complicated. The trick is to keep your personal values in mind, stay centred and block out the everyday noise.

In this book, I'll share the simple strategies I've used to help dozens of people set up a financial system that works for them and is matched to their stage of life, their tolerance for risk and, most importantly, their personal values. When it comes to planning your financial future, the biggest mistake you can make is to keep your head in the sand. If you fail to plan, you're planning to fail.

This book is your opportunity to grow and realise your financial and lifestyle goals. Then you can be one of the few who can live life according to your truth. We will discuss the ways you can achieve both your financial and lifestyle goals, according to a process I call the '5Cs of Financial Planning': Clarify, Calibrate, Construct, Create and Continue. Without covering these areas, no one is likely to achieve outcomes they desire for their short-, medium- and long-term benefit.

It all begins with being accountable to the present at an individual level. Progression, love, reverence and prosperity are all inside jobs. It's a basic human need to feel safe and appreciated, and to contribute. Rarely is there anything 'new' in finance; the only thing that is new is our openness to learn and view things differently.

The Tao of Wealth and Prosperity is about aligning your finances with your values. It will challenge you to think differently about your prospects and wealth creation, showing you how to build prosperity and capital so you can be money-smart, grow a business and still live a good and fulfilling life.

PART ONE
FUNDAMENTALS

1
The Role Of A
Trusted Advisor

These days, a financial advisor can be a lot more than someone who gives you stock tips. While all financial advisors have legally binding fiduciary responsibilities to put your interests first, only some will go the extra mile to get to know you and your goals and values.

In this chapter, we'll look at the role and responsibilities of a financial advisor, what to look for in an advisor and the financial goals associated with four stages in life. I'll introduce you to my streamlined system for achieving financial success: the 5Cs. We'll also look at how a truly great advisor will take the time to understand your core values and life goals to ensure your plans are a perfect fit for your world view.

Responsibilities of a financial advisor

The role of a financial advisor is to help a client achieve their financial and lifestyle goals. Financial advisors have a legal responsibility to act in their client's best interests and, unlike a broker, they must disclose their financial strategy and legally prove that the advice they provide is going to place a client in a better position.

Financial advisors have come a long way, and despite recent history with the Hayne Royal Commission into Misconduct in the Banking, Superannuation and Financial Services Industry and multiple independent inquiries into the financial services sector, they are still a vital part of Australia's economy and have the capacity to service the people in their community.

A fitting analogy for the importance of fiduciary operations to the economy can be found in the duodenum. The economy, like the human body, is made of multiple organs, each of which serves a purpose. The major organs of the economy are the banking sector, government, households, firms and international trade – like the human body has a heart, lungs, brain, skin and intestine. Two of the most essential organs of the human body are also among the smallest – our eyes and our duodenum. These are like the roles of the entrepreneur and the fiduciary, who pull various small but important levers within the economy.

We'll take a look at the entrepreneur – the 'eyes' – in Chapter 7, but for now let's examine the duodenum. This is the first section of the small intestine, connected to the stomach and acting as a conduit between the gall bladder, liver and pancreas to prepare digested food for the rest of the intestine. The function of the duodenum is to neutralise stomach acids, which in turn allows the intestine to process the nutrients of food more easily and prevents harm to the digestive tract.

A fiduciary duty is a legal relationship between two (sometimes more) parties, where one party (the fiduciary) promises the other party (the client, called the principal) to act solely in their interest. This duty is the highest level of care expected by the law.

Fiduciaries must:

1. Place the principal's interest before their own and be extremely loyal to the person to whom they owe the duty

2. Not enter into arrangements that give rise to conflict between their own interest and the interest of the principal

3. Not profit from the position unless the principal provides informed consent[1]

---

1   Financial Planning Association of Australia, *The Pillars of Our Profession: Code of professional practice* (FPA, Sydney, 2015), https://fpa.com.au/wp-content/uploads/2015/09/FPA_CodeofPractice_July2013.pdf, accessed 4 January 2021

Transformation of the financial industry

Financial advisors have a fiduciary duty to their principals. The industry has come a long way since its birth when financial advisors were simply insurance salespeople knocking on doors. Gone are the days of pseudo stockbrokers trying to pick winners.

Banking and financial services have gone through multiple iterations in recent memory, such as the Future of Financial Advice reforms in 2012[2] and culminating in the Hayne Royal Commission into Misconduct in the Banking, Superannuation and Financial Services Industry.[3] Perspective is a wonderful gift that we can only bestow upon ourselves, and in the business world, it's a lot easier to understand things with the gift of hindsight.

In the future, financial advisors will operate in a similar way to lawyers and solicitors with an attuned understanding of economics, tax and finance. Advisors will always have to contend with 'conflicted remuneration' as they are remunerated for their services. But unlike a broker, who is incentivised to sell as much as he or she can and has no responsibilities for the outcomes, an advisor will have to be completely transparent in how he or she discloses remuneration and services.

---

2   https://asic.gov.au/regulatory-resources/financial-services/
    regulatory-reforms/future-of-financial-advice-fofa-reforms
3   www.financialservices.royalcommission.gov.au

Barbers and surgeons

The financial industry is not the only sector that has evolved legal responsibilities to serve the interests of its clients. Take, for example, the barber-surgeons of the Middle Ages. There is a reason the barber's pole is coloured red, white and blue, and it's not a tribute to Americana; it's far more grotesque.[4]

The story of barbers and surgeons stems from the divergence of monks.[5] Let's take a look.

Due to the rules and laws of a monastery, Catholic monks had to maintain a tonsure (shaved hair on the crown). This in turn created a need for barbers, who became the only people in the monastery who had access to razors and equipment that could shave another monk's hair.

The local monks were also charged with medicinal and surgical obligations in times of war and mass sickness. It was the barber-surgeons who filled the void of specialised medical practitioners and were responsible for amputating limbs and performing tooth extractions, though they had no expertise in this field and no specialised skills.

---

4   N Lee, 'Here's the disturbing reason why barber poles are red, white, and blue' (*Business Insider*, 29 June 2017) www.businessinsider.com.au/disturbing-reason-barber-poles-red-white-blue-2017-6?r=US&IR=T

5   R Milnes Walker, 'The barber surgeons of Bristol, *Bristol Medico-Chirurgical Journal*, 90:18 (September 1975), pp51–56

It wasn't until 1163 at the Council of Tours that the Catholic Church made a clear distinction between physicians and barbers, thus creating a pedigree of expertise.[6] The divergence of barbers and surgeons today couldn't be more profound. It takes years of elite training and education to become a surgeon,[7] while barbers and hairdressers have a skilled trade. But the pole outside a barber shop remains as a literal representation of the tort and malpractice from hundreds of years ago (blood – red; amputated limbs – blue; bandages – white).

Like the barber-surgeons, financial advisors once offered a grab bag of different services, from insurance salespeople to stockbrokers. But in recent years, financial advisors have specialised and diversified, so it pays to know what you're looking for. You don't want to hire a barber when you need a surgeon.

What to look for in a financial advisor

When choosing a financial advisor (planner), ensure that at a minimum they:

- Have a Certified Financial Planners qualification and membership to the Financial Planners Association (the highest and most rigorous designation an advisor can achieve)

6   L Himmelmann, 'Från barberare till chirurgie magister – steg på vägen mot en läkarprofession' [From barber to surgeon – the process of professionalization], *Sven Med Tidskr*, 11:1 (2007), pp69–87
7   D Watters, 'Guy de Chauliac: pre-eminent surgeon of the Middle Ages', *ANZ Journal of Surgery*, 83:10 (6 June 2013)

- Are a representative of or hold an Australian Financial Services Licence (this will be found in a Financial Services Guide)

- Explain their remuneration, fees and range of ongoing service packages up front

However, a financial advisor can be a lot more than someone who ticks the legal boxes. A truly great advisor helps you align your financial plans with your core values.

Life stages

A good financial advisor will take the time to gain an excellent understanding of you – your values, your goals and your current stage in life. The last point is important because your financial objectives will vary enormously according to each of your life stages.

I've broken up financial goals according to four key life stages:

1. **Starting out** – new entrants into the workforce, wanting to get ahead on their financial journey and save for their first home

2. **Sorting it out** – a married couple with a young family, looking to fill their house with warmth and security by putting 'everything together' and perhaps saving for their children's education

3. **Branching out** – a middle-aged couple or business owner, looking to create more time in their busy schedule and wanting more holidays with their children, build on their capital and expand their options so that they can semi-retire before the standard age of sixty-five

4. **Getting out** – a client who is approaching retirement and looking to make sure that they continue to live with purpose and their capital lasts well and truly into their golden years

Each of these life stages revolves around a different set of goals. Common examples of client goals are to:

- Pay off my mortgage

- Buy a house/investment property

- Pay for my child's education

- Prepare in case of unexpected illness or events

- Feel secure about my finances in retirement/not be a burden to my family as I grow older

- Feel secure about my finances now

- Leave an inheritance to my loved ones

- Protect my business's stakeholders (shareholders)

- Invest a sum of money in line with an agreed asset allocation

There is an art to having clarity in your goals. What separates a goal from a wish is whether it is specific, measurable, achievable, realistic and time-bound (SMART). It's also a matter of how you articulate and prioritise your goals. There's a sharp distinction between a vague goal and a SMART goal. A vague goal might be something like 'I wish to retire on an income of $80,000 per annum by the time I am sixty-five'. A trusted advisor will be able to help you turn your vague goals into SMART goals, something more like these:

For someone starting out – 'I wish to buy my mother's home in the Blue Mountains. She is approaching retirement and I want to enter the property market. I would like to save for a deposit of $180,000 in five years' time, purchase the home for $650,000 and ensure that my mother can retire on her own terms.'

For a couple sorting it out – 'We're looking to buy our first home and start a family. We wish for our household to be safe and happy, so that our children can attend a great school, which we believe will cost around $20,000 per annum, per child. We wish to be mortgage free ($700,000) by the time our kids graduate Year 12. For our family to be protected, we wish to have security and peace of mind, knowing that if something were to happen to either one of us, they would be provided for. And we've got $1 million of life insurance and disablement cover to clear our mortgage and pay the school fees, and have each got $100,000 of critical-illness cover in the event of a medical emergency. Our income is protected for $80,000 per annum until retirement at sixty-five. That way, neither one of us as a parent is precluded from retiring on our own terms.'

For a business owner branching out – 'I wish to take a backward step from working in the business to be working on the business. I would like to have two weeks of extra holiday a year with my family, which will cost me $30,000 per holiday. I wish to start generating alternative assets and capital that will allow me to semi-retire in five years' time, be mortgage free and have a sufficient retirement capital of $2 million by the time I am sixty, which will generate an income of $90,000 per annum. To achieve this, I need to develop a succession plan and immediately perform a stakeholder analysis.

'In the event of my incapacity, I wish to ensure the business will continue and be able to fulfil my wishes. This may include life, disability and critical-illness cover. I wish to ensure that the company's balance sheet remains protected and that there is a replacement for me who will continue generating profit of $X to the business's shareholders.'

For someone getting out – 'I wish to retire to my holiday home by the beach in Nelson Bay by the time I am sixty. My family can then visit me there on the weekend or for summer holidays. I wish to have a capital base of at least $1.6 million to cover my expenses of $80,000 per year and help my children and grandchildren enjoy quality time together. I wish to help them into the property market and with school fees wherever possible.'

The 5Cs of Financial Planning

It is ingrained in the human psyche to think short term. As a financial advisor, I help my clients shift their thinking to the long term and focus on their future self in ten years' time. Financial literacy is not a side effect of wealth; wealth is a side effect of financial literacy.

I've designed the process to ensure that my clients enjoy safe harbour provisions (as set out in the Future of Financial Advice reforms[8] and in line with the Corporations Act 2012[9]) to act in their best interest according to the principles of the 5Cs of Financial Planning: Clarify, Calibrate, Construct, Create, Continue.

Clarify

Gaining clarity on turning the intangible into something that you can see and measure is the foundation

---

8   *Future of Financial Advice: Best interests duty and related obligation* (ASIC, Brisbane, 2012), http://download.asic.gov.au/media/2125918/rg175-ris.pdf, accessed 14 January 2021
9   https://asic.gov.au/regulatory-resources/financial-services/regulatory-reforms/future-of-financial-advice-fofa-reforms

for success. Achieving your goals is a matter of how you prioritise and budget for your vision. People often fail when there are competing goals and priorities,[10] leaving them stuck in the same place or ruing missed opportunities.

A certified financial planner will be able to outline all the benefits and risks of all financial decisions that are commonly made. They can raise your awareness about the mistakes that people can easily make, which in turn end up costing time and money.

Due to the abundance of information on the internet, everyone seems to have an opinion, and as a result people who are uninformed can be easily influenced, misled and fall into traps. In the Clarify stage, I take the time to ensure I have a good understanding of my client's goals and values and open up a dialogue about their financial future, ensuring they are aware of the benefits and the risks.

Calibrate

To be financially centred, you have to have the tools at your disposal to achieve your goals. A builder may not blame his or her tools for their work, but she or he still needs tools to build a home.

---

10 A Duckworth, JJ Gross, 'Self-control and grit: Related but separable determinants of success', *Current Directions in Psychological Science*, 23 (2014), pp319–25

This step of the process is about research. During the Calibrate step, I research my client's current situation and ensure that any recommendations I make are not cost-prohibitive to their goals and any products that they have are still fit for purpose or to the standard they require.

This is the time to consider whether you are investing in the right type of entities and have made necessary considerations to minimise your tax. A financial advisor isn't a tax specialist like your accountant, but they can certainly acknowledge and provide some foresight into how to structure your affairs appropriately in accordance with the law and in a manner that prevents you 'painting yourself into a corner'. It's vitally important for your financial advisor and your accountant to work together – the advisor provides the advice and the strategy, receiving guidance from the accountant. The accountant then implements the entities and makes sure everything is compliant with requirements.

Your advisor should also measure your tolerance and capacity for investment risk and ensure that it is aligned to your goals. Should insurance feature in any of the advice, an advisor can research whether your current product is fit for purpose or talk to underwriters for a pre-assessment of your current health status.

The Calibrate step involves the advisor performing the necessary behind-the-scenes tasks that demonstrate best interest duty on behalf of clients.

Construct

When constructing a portfolio, I adhere to the fundamental principle that you always go into an investment for profit and to make money *first*. Can a financial advisor help you get better returns? The simple answer is yes.

It does depend on mitigating factors such as timing and how much risk you wish to take, but it is the job of a financial advisor to improve returns or make adjustments to a portfolio where necessary. While returns are important, the basis of your relationship with your financial advisor is built upon doing the right thing and making prudent and sound decisions.

At this stage of the journey, I put together a proposal that outlines the scope of advice and confirm my client's goals and objectives. I use three acronyms to make sure my client's interests are covered from all angles: GREAT, SWEAT and TIME.

When considering an investment philosophy, as a financial advisor, I make sure that a portfolio is GREAT:

• Goal aligned

• Risk addressed

- Explore your options

- Asset allocation agreed

- Time considered

Investing shouldn't be considered in isolation, particularly if you are in a position where family members or stakeholders depend on you. Insurance is a prudent and important consideration as black swan events (ie surprises) do occur. Insurance prevents any losses so you can continue to weather a storm.

In these times of hardship, is your wealth and balance sheet going to SWEAT? Consider whether you have sufficient:

- Savings

- Welfare (government benefits)

- Estate (the bank of Mum and Dad)

- Assets to realise

- Time to recover

There are always trade-offs which could impact your estate and beneficiaries. Considerations to make in this due process are a matter of TIME:

- Tax consequences

- Investing for beneficiaries

- Managing your affairs (avoiding intestacy)

- Executor

Approximately 50% of Australians have a will, the other half of estates have to be administered by intestacy, ie the State Trustee. It's important to consider what forms a part of an estate and what else to take into account. A financial advisor can provide you with guidance and strategy on your estate, but you also need to consult with a professional estate planning lawyer in conjunction with your solicitor.

Create

All personal recommendations made by a financial advisor must be outlined in a document called a Statement of Advice, or financial plan. This plan outlines the strategy or road map to create your financial future.

These documents are lengthy in nature but contain all the information about you and your goals. A Statement of Advice contains strategy recommendations, product recommendations, an alternate strategy and cash-flow modelling that will show you what the future looks like. Legally, financial advisors are not allowed to give any recommendations for a product, investment or strategy unless it is documented in a Statement of Advice.

Continue

A financial plan is only as good as its execution and implementation. As well as markets, circumstances are always subject to change. Maintain your relationship with your advisor on a review basis to ensure that you remain on track and informed, so you can have confidence that your welfare and livelihood remain secure.

According to Russell Investments' 2019 *Value of an Advisor Study*, the full value of a financial advisor's services extends 'beyond investment-only advice – at a minimum of 4.4 per cent of investible funds, with the avoidance of behavioural mistakes providing the lion's share of value'.[11]

The Tao of financial advice

Being a financial advisor is a privilege. It is more difficult and complex than some people may imagine, especially as it involves a delicate and trusting relationship with a client. It also involves entering another person's 'circle'[12] where they are entrusting you with their money in a world full of uncertainty.

---

11   *Value: Why work with a financial advisor?* (Russell Investments, 2019), https://russellinvestments.com/Publications/US/Document/2019_Value_of_Advisor_EI.pdf, accessed 14 January 2021
12   W Mischel, *The Marshmallow Test: Understanding self-control and how to master it* (Penguin Random House, London, 2014)

I've always taken this role very seriously. The role of financial advisor is part advisor, part mentor and part coach. A good financial advisor motivates and inspires you to pursue your dreams, and instils discipline and willpower when that's what you need. He or she is the person you can turn to when the confusion and competing voices all around you threaten to obscure your goals.

Alice in Wonderland

From a financial planning perspective, clients who pay too much attention to the media over-emphasise the recency of current affairs, and can in turn make decisions that are going to cost them money, time and emotional distress. There will always be a gap between the stock market and the real economy, and the media love to play devil's advocate.

To illustrate this, I'd like to draw your attention to some of the messages from the story of *Alice in Wonderland*. In many respects, it comments on current affairs and our ability to make decisions.

As with all young children, curiosity tended to get the better of Alice. Bored by her mother's teachings, she spotted a white rabbit dressed in a red jacket frantically racing across the meadow. Curiosity is often followed by trouble. Following Rabbit down the warren, Alice fell through the centre of the earth and opened the doors to Wonderland.

During her journey in Wonderland, Alice becomes lost in the forest and encounters the Cheshire Cat. The Cat takes her to the Rabbit's house and the Mad Hatter's tea party, both of which lead in turn to the Red Queen's garden, another incomprehensible place. Alice is overwhelmed, lost and confused, struggling to come to terms with her own moral authority in light of everyone else's madness.

In the eyes of a child, *Alice in Wonderland* is fantastic, thrilling and exciting. But something more sinister lurks under the surface – a mad and tangled array of conflicting information.

These days, our smartphones allow us to have access to a 'Wonderland' in our hip-pockets. It shouldn't come as a surprise that we struggle to regulate our emotions and can often be drawn to extreme archetypes of hedonism or nihilism. Becoming more susceptible and impressionable and projecting our views onto others is unhealthy. In this age of constantly checking our phones (every twelve minutes on average), it's no wonder rates of anxiety and depression are becoming more prevalent.

If you follow the changing tides of headlines and Google searches, nearly every second day you will find something that will predict the next crash or spooky implications of another fractious geopolitical tension. In other words, you'll be just like Alice, ping-ponging from one mad situation to the next. Tech and social-media companies purposely socially engineer their users to be hooked on engagement: that's why the story of *Alice in Wonderland* has relevance to our lives in this period in history.

When we examine the story as adults, we can see some telling metaphors in the main characters:

- A media commentator pontificates about nationalistic values, pointing the blame at someone who clashes with their opinion while pandering to the influence of a media oligarch (Rabbit).

- Donald Trump tweets (Mad Queen).

- The endearing influencer tries to sell the latest fad about a dietary supplement (Cheshire Cat).

- Some 'overly idealistic militant socialist' virtue signals in Facebook's comments section (Mad Hatter).

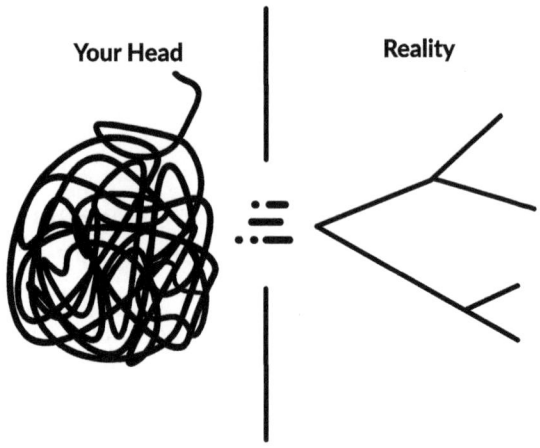

When you look at the markets over a long time, they are far more stable and reliable than the latest social-media buzz. Over the past 120 years, the world has survived two wars, two pandemics, the Global Financial Crash and the Great Depression, while still being able to innovate and bounce back.

Alice in Wonderland is a story of adolescence. Alice constantly grows and shrinks in size throughout the story, which is symbolic of the innocence of a young girl struggling to come to terms with her own maturity and projecting her morals onto a world of nonsense. Nobody around her listens, and yet she must defend her values against the opinions and consequences of other people who are literally all mad.

People can lose themselves in current events or competing for approval on the internet. We can get absorbed in the headlines which prevent us from making a decision and deprive us of opportunity. That's when the trusted voice of a financial advisor who knows and understands our personal values can be worth its weight in gold.

Summary

In this chapter, we've covered the fiduciary responsibilities of financial advisors and how far the industry has come since the days of door-to-door insurance salesmen. We've looked at the ways that a truly great financial advisor will go beyond the legal requirements to understand your core values and life goals so they can steer a course for you through a complex landscape that can sometimes feel as mad as Wonderland. We've looked at the different kinds of financial goals that people typically set at different life stages and how to clarify those goals along SMART principles. Finally, we looked at the 5Cs of my personal system of financial planning: Clarify, Calibrate, Construct, Create and Continue. These five steps have helped dozens of people to set and achieve financial goals they never dreamed possible.

If you wish to know more about your financial strengths to create a better future, view my scorecard at https://financialstrengthsscorecard.scoreapp.com or scan the QR code below.

2
Operating A Budget

The fundamental premises of budgeting are pay yourself first and spend less than you earn. A successful budget is one that strips away the things that are non-essential and compartmentalises your spending habits by keeping things automated and simple. Your ability to budget will determine your success in wealth creation, and consistency will enable you to achieve your financial goals and objectives and ensure your future happiness.

Your daily habits can strongly influence your long-term financial success. Money is a medium of exchange and a store of value. The core of budgeting is to focus on building capital – being cash-flow poor and equity rich is the best way to achieve your goals.

In this chapter, we'll look at the shift in mindset it takes to start focusing on equity rather than income and the common ways in which people fail to maintain budget discipline. We'll also look at the three pots of successful budgeting and the six accounts – I call them the 'Six Guardians of the Galaxy' – that you can establish to keep your budget goals on track. Finally, we'll examine the importance of infusing your budget with your own values to ensure that you make space for the people and passions that fuel your happiness: the Tao of budgeting.

The apple doesn't fall far from the tree

There's a science to budgeting that requires a shift in thinking about what money is and how it works. If you apply a scientific method to reconciling a budget from your bank statement, your chances of financial success will dramatically increase. To do this, it's important you understand the difference between income and capital.

Think of the story about Sir Isaac Newton recognising the existence of gravity. On a picture-perfect English summer's day, he was sitting under an apple tree in Trinity College, Cambridge and an apple dropped to his side. Newton then had an epiphany, which in turn led to the discovery of the general theory of gravity and the three laws of motion.

You can think of money like Newton's apple tree. The fruit (apple) is income and the capital is the tree. It's a shift in thinking where you're forced to focus not just on cash flow, but also on building capital, or growing the tree. In the long run, you're always going to be better off being cash-flow poor and asset or equity rich. That is to say, it's not about how much money you make; it's how you make your money. The apple doesn't fall far from the tree and an apple a day keeps your financial doctor (advisor) away.

As with Newton's laws of motion, budgeting has three laws:

- Law number 1 – align your present and future self by saving and spending on positively nourishing activities that enhance your financial, spiritual, emotional and physical needs.

- Law number 2 – divide your budget into needs, investments (and insurances) and wants.

- Law number 3 – focus on building capital (save to invest, don't just save to save).

CATHY'S STORY

Take the example of a recent client of mine. Cathy was a single mum doing her best to make ends meet. She and her daughter had never received much help, the only form being the sisterhood of local single mums who took care of one another. Like many single mums, Cathy was struggling financially.

On the surface, Cathy put on a big positive front. Underneath it all, though, was a girl who needed a hug and, in her words, a manicure (joke).

Cathy's goal was to provide a better future for her daughter. She valued her own independence and wanted to feel treasured, loved and safe, giving her the confidence to raise a happy and competent daughter. Asking for help at first seemed a stretch, but given her situation and the scope of advice, I was happy to share my time by going through a budget with her.

Cathy came to me overwhelmed and uncertain; a better life for both herself and her daughter seemed a distant dream. Even though she had two jobs, between her daughter's day care and essentials for the home, there was still little money left over at the end of the week.

'I stress about money, so to relieve myself of stress, I take myself shopping, which only leads to more stress about money,' she told me. 'Then I get stressed about having to be stressed.' It was a cycle that was hard to break and added to a growing credit-card debt.

Engaging with Cathy taught me a valuable lesson in humanity: treat everyone as an individual and respect their situation, because you don't know what they are going through. We went through her bank account and prioritised what was essential: rent, food, clothes and some small treats that were going to keep Cathy and her daughter sane. After taking out some of the unnecessary items, we found there was some cash left over.

Funnily enough, we discovered that the money she was earning at her second job equated to the amount she was paying in after-school care for her daughter.

The income and the expenses of day care ended up cancelling each other out, so she quit her second job and gained more quality time with her daughter.

Today we still keep in touch, not as an advisor and client, but as mates. Despite her financial troubles, Cathy is still able to make everyone smile and is grateful for every moment with her daughter, whether it is good or bad. The credit-card debt has now been erased and her daughter has started high school top of the class. Better yet, each year, Cathy is able to save for a Christmas holiday, time together for just the two of them.

The seven seductive sins

As you can see from Cathy's story, sometimes you can make savings in areas where you least expect it. While there is much focus on being wealthy, it's also important to focus on what you can eliminate from your budget. Former Navy Seal Commander Jocko Willink embraces the mantra of 'discipline equals freedom'.[13] Not everyone gets to be a Navy Seal and hunt down terrorists, but sometimes the best advice is not necessarily what to do, but what to stop and kill.

These are what I call 'the seven seductive sins':

1. Cigarettes and too much alcohol

2. Too much unnecessary tax

---

13 J Willink, L Babin, *Extreme Ownership: How US Navy SEALS lead and win* (St Martins Press, New York, 2015)

3. People who waste your time and energy

4. Fast food and too many takeaways

5. Gambling

6. Unused subscriptions

7. Lingering credit-card debt

If you want to pinpoint your expenditure precisely and track your expenses, you can download the budget planner from the resources page at www.equanimityfs.com.au/resources. A good financial advisor should be able to offer you an automated system that links to your credit card(s) and bank accounts and demonstrates where your expenditure is. It's important that you focus on what's essential.[14]

TANYA'S STORY

It's not only the seven seductive sins that can play havoc with your budget; any kind of spending can get out of hand if you don't keep an eye on it.

I can recall a time when I was an associate advisor working with a senior partner. One of his clients was a high-profile lawyer – let's call her Tanya – who was earning a serious income of about $500,000 per annum. The trouble was, Tanya couldn't save a cent! In one year, she spent $56,000 on Ubers to and from her workplace. Despite our advice and warnings, her spending got so

---

14   G McKeown, *Essentialism: The disciplined pursuit of less* (Virgin Books, London, 2014)

out of hand that she even had to sell an investment property inside her superannuation fund and withdraw from her husband's account-based pension to keep up her mortgage repayments.

The lesson – it's not necessarily what you earn, but what you spend it on that matters. It's all about maintaining focus. The single biggest mistake Tanya and many other people make when it comes to building wealth is that they do not track their expenses.

The best way to implement and execute on your budget is to have everything automated. Then you can focus on the things that are going to generate the most joy and energy for you.

Three pots

A great way to budget is to compartmentalise your expenditure into three distinct pots. One pot is for your needs, the second is to invest and insure yourself and the third to splurge and treat yourself in the present moment.

Pot 1 – Needs = 50%

We all need food, shelter, time to recover and company. Focus on what's essential and on quality, not quantity. There's a correlation between wealth and health; in this regard you're allowed to be selfish.

The best way to think of this is ME:

- Minimal

- Essential

When you're purchasing items that are basic needs, direct your focus on those that are going to boost your energy and vitality. Human beings have an uncanny ability to adapt to new circumstances and are built for change, but this requires nutrition and sustenance. Our vitality is dependent on our daily habits which can be boiled down to the food we consume, the amount of sleep we get and how well we stay hydrated.[15] This ultimately affects our health, mood and performance.

Pot 2 – Investments and insurances = 25%

The second pot is for you to set aside money for your investments and insurances. There are always going to be times of economic summer, autumn, winter and spring – it's best to plant trees now so that you can cater for all seasons. In later chapters, we will discuss building capital by investing and protecting it with insurance, but for the time being, just remember the rule of thumb: it is best to be cash-flow poor and equity rich. The truest measure of wealth is what's in your asset column, not your earnings.

---

15   T Corley, *Change Your Habits, Change Your Life: Strategies that transformed 177 average people into self-made millionaires* (North Loop Books, Minneapolis, 2016), p9

Keep in mind when you're aligning a budget with your long-term goals that making sacrifices in the present will allow the fruits of your labour to appreciate in value. If you are relying purely on your salary for your finances, like Grasshopper in the story below, you are one step away from poverty.

THE ANT AND THE GRASSHOPPER

The story of the Ant and the Grasshopper in *Aesop's Fables*[16] is about the decisions we make in life, which are not just confined to money, investing or retirement planning. In the story, throughout the summer, the Ant stores away food for the winter while the Grasshopper lives a life of self-indulgence.

Lo and behold, come winter, the Grasshopper is struggling for survival while the Ant has a labyrinth of places to live in the ground, away from the harsh winter, and enough food to survive until the spring.

Like the Grasshopper, we humans often struggle to associate our present self with our future self.[17] If you feel closely connected to your future self, you will be more likely to take into account how your present actions will impact how you feel later. Take a look at the picture below. Where do you currently feel you are aligned to?

16 *Æsop Fables*, retold by Joseph Jacobs. *Harvard Classics* Vol 17:1. www.bartleby.com / 17 / 1, accessed 28 October 2020

17 W Mischel *The Marshmallow Test: Understanding self-control and how to master it* (Penguin Random House, London, 2014)

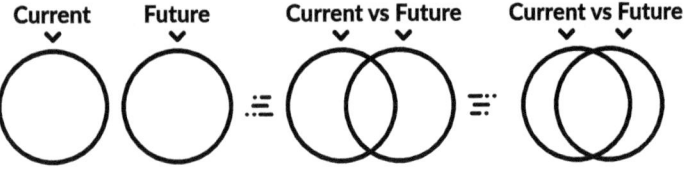

Pot 3 – Wants = 25%

Establishing a budget is also about creating space to do the things that light you up. There's no benefit in being the richest person in the graveyard! The most important thing with aligning your goals to the things that you want in life is to ensure your budget is in line with your priorities. This could be spending more time with loved ones or making provision for things that are going to enable you to grow spiritually and emotionally. Spend your time and money with the people who elevate you and give you energy (even if you're an introvert).

Money is there to be used, and yes, from time to time you are allowed to enjoy yourself. It is possible to still be ambitious and enjoy your life; you don't need to stick with an antiquated belief that you're not allowed time to yourself in the fear of being called lazy.[18] When it comes to your wants, focus your expenditure on what is going to spark joy and form memories. There

---

18 J Hibberd, *The Imposter Cure: How to stop feeling like a fraud and escape the mind-trap of imposter syndrome* (Octopus Publishing Group, London, 2019)

are times where you deserve the holiday or a nice dinner out – the juice is all the sweeter when it is earnt.

The Six Guardians of the Galaxy

To get your budgeting on track, I suggest you follow the bank account of the Six Guardians of the Galaxy:

1. Credit card for all your direct debits, including subscriptions, insurances and memberships, which is cleared at the end of each month.

2. Expense account for groceries, food and entertainment – this can be topped up each week.

3. A high-interest savings account – your rainy-day fund for any unexpected expenses (a trip to the doctor or car breakdown).

4. A transactional account that links to all of your investments in a share or wrap platform and any extra superannuation contributions.

5. Joint account (or offset) for your rent or mortgage repayments.

6. Line of credit for investing (optional).

The Tao of budgeting

While providing advice to exercise physiologists and allied-health professionals, I have noticed an alignment between our values and effects. In healthcare, small proactive steps towards your daily physical health and mental wellbeing compound over time, and eventually take the stress load off the health system. As a financial advisor, I assist people to focus their needs into four categories:

1. Financial

2. Spiritual

3. Emotional

4. Physical

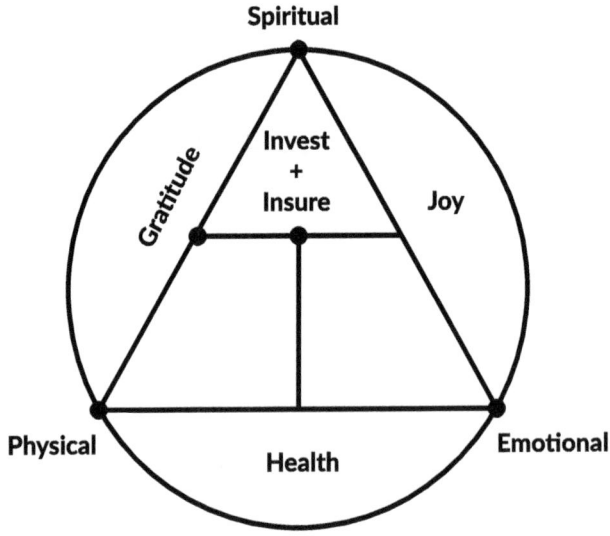

One trick with budgeting is to look beyond the figures and search for where you are spending your energy.

In their book *The Power of Full Engagement*,[19] Jim Loehr and Tony Schwartz emphasise the importance of rituals. Sometimes our energy is exhausted simply by having too much choice. More choice can actually make us less satisfied. The implications for our daily lives are that too many choices are bad for our mental health and diminish our happiness.

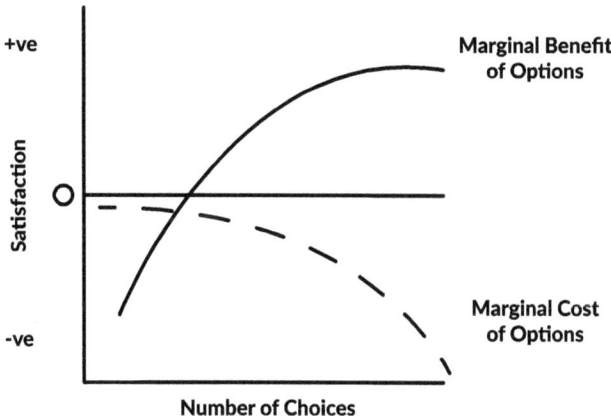

A similar phenomenon affects money and happiness – we can reach a certain tipping point where earning more money does not make us happier. The magic number is about $80,000 per annum; after that, our rate of happiness starts to plateau. In other words, for every $1 extra we earn over this threshold, we don't become happier; we remain the same up until about $200,000. Then we actually become less happy, and the curve is shaped rather like an inverted horseshoe.

19 JE Loehr, T Schwartz, *The Power of Full Engagement: Managing energy, not time, is the key to high performance and personal renewal* (Free Press, New York, 2003)

And there's often a curse to the long hours it takes to make this money: we never get to see our family or relish time spent with friends.

Why is this? When the benefits of wealth are more accessible, they lose meaning. Another sports car or new toy becomes just that: *another* new car; *another* new toy. We can have a polished sports car and still be unfulfilled on the inside: the novelty eventually wears off and we have no time to spend with the people we care about.

Our time here on earth is limited, so spending time with loved ones and creating memories is important, no matter how big or small the cherry on top of earning lots of money may be. Spend quality time with people who are going to give you good energy. A belly laugh, happiness and abundance are the antidotes to sadness and worry, and will usually bring you more joy than a fat bank account.

Summary

If you're not in a position where you would like to be financially, it's likely this can be traced to your capacity to save or increase your earnings. Having a budget in place will cater to your financial, emotional, spiritual and health needs. The life you end up with is an accumulation of the choices you make. They can deliver you to your goals or send you spiralling off to a galaxy far away.

In this chapter, we've looked at the difference between diverting money towards income and assets, and the common ways that you can be derailed from your goals. We also looked at three pots you can divide your money into for successful budgeting: 50% for needs, 25% for investment and insurances and 25% for wants. We looked at the Six Guardians of the Galaxy accounts that can help you achieve your budget goals, and at the importance of ensuring that your budget aligns with your inner values and doesn't prioritise wealth over happiness: the Tao of budgeting.

Should you wish to plan a budget and reconcile your bank statement, you can download a free copy of a budget planner from the resources page at www.equanimityfs.com.au / resources.

3
Insurance And Estate Planning

Discussions about insurance and estate planning can sometimes bring up difficult emotions. After all, this is when we must think about protecting ourselves and our loved ones against undesirable outcomes, such as illness, injury and death. But these are important conversations.

In this chapter, we will learn to think like a Navy diver when it comes to insurance and estate planning: with confidence, calm and clarity. We'll also look at the kinds of insurances available and how they may or may not apply to your personal circumstances, plus how a financial advisor can assist in navigating you through these issues. We'll examine the particulars of business insurance and the importance of keeping it all in perspective.

If you consider insurance and estate planning from a Tao perspective, you'll understand that they are ultimately about safeguarding the future of the ones you love most.

The clarity of a Navy diver

The Australian Navy clearance diving unit is one of the most esteemed special forces units in the world. The function of a Navy clearance diver is simple: go into a hostile territory, survey the enemy and remove any hazards that compromise the mission. Common duties involve the disposal of improvised explosive devices (mines) which could cause death or damage ships. Other duties involve dealing with people seeking asylum and refuge. It is the obligation of divers to treat each refugee who is in a compromised position of vulnerability as an individual, with integrity and the utmost respect.

In situations where vessels may be endangered and conditions unfavourable, divers must exude confidence, clarity of thought and calmness. Their priority must be saving human lives and assuring a safe haven. Working in a high-performance team where lives are at stake, a clearance diver must be ready for any circumstance to unfold and prepare for the worst-case scenario.

We can learn from this calm preparedness when we approach our own financial planning. Our lives may not require us to face anything as dangerous as clearing mines, but we all face our challenges. As Mike Tyson famously said, 'Everyone has a plan until they get punched in the mouth.' If there is one lesson the COVID-19 crisis has taught us, it's that unexpected events can and do occur a lot more often than we may like to think.

Our human capital and intellectual property are the things that generate wealth and opportunity for our future. As our earning capacity is intrinsically linked to the amount of energy we have, an expected event (such as our passing, sickness or incapacity) can prove disastrous to our family's welfare and livelihood. Our natural instincts and biases lead us to believe 'it won't happen to me', but the reality is that the rear-view mirror is a lot clearer than the windshield, and the path forward will always be uncertain and beyond our control.

The importance of insurance and insurance advice

There is an estimated $1.88 billion underinsurance gap in Australia, according to a Clearview whitepaper on Advice Culture and Remuneration, a citation of Rice Warner's report on Australia's Underinsurance Gap.[20]

---

20 *Advice Culture and Remuneration* (ClearView, Sydney, 2019), www.clearview.com.au/documents/ebooks/Commissions-whitepaper-June-2019/Commissions-Report-whitepaper, accessed 4 January 2021

In a submission to the Productivity Commission on 23 August 2017, Rice Warner showed:

- The levels of default cover have provided valuable insurance for most working Australians

- Default levels of insurance cover do not inappropriately erode the retirement savings of most members

- The extent to which life insurance cover offsets costs to Government in the form of reduced social security payments

According to the Australian Prudential Regulation Authority (APRA) Life Insurance Claims and Disputes statistics (27 June 2019), individually advised policies showed a higher admittance rate (96%) compared to individually non-advised (88%).[21] The discrepancy in admittance rate could be because people who received some form of advice were better informed about what they were covered for, compared to the uncertainty of relying on research when purchasing insurance directly. Advised policies are generally fully underwritten, as opposed to non-advised policies that are generally not underwritten or only partially underwritten at application time. Because of this, direct policies can have a wide range of exclusions compared to insurance purchased via an intermediary (advised).

---

21 R Cain, 'Life insurance claims statistics in Australia' (Life Insurance Direct, 2020), www.lifeinsurancedirect.com.au/life-insurance-claims-statistics-australia, accessed 14 January 2021

Kinds of insurance

It is prudent in financial planning to always consider a worst-case scenario and an exit strategy. This is the reason for insurance in a family or business portfolio of investments. An insurance policy is a forward-looking contract where you as the individual have your life insured and pay a premium to the insurer in advance to protect yourself against potential loss for a given event.

Let's now discuss the most common forms of insurance handled by your financial advisor.

Term-life insurance

A lump-sum payment made to a beneficiary in the event of the insured person's passing, or in some cases when the person insured has been given two years to live. These policies can be standalone in your name or held within your superannuation fund.

Total permanent disablement (TPD) insurance

Passing away is not the only thing to prepare for. TPD insurance is important for the cost of care over many years in the event of total and permanent disablement. There are three definitions of TPD insurance:

- **Own Occupation** – where an insured person is unlikely ever to follow their occupation in the event of a claim. These are suited to professionals with specialised skills such as a surgeon or barrister. An Own Occupation policy must be paid from your personal bank account.

- **Any Occupation** – a lump-sum payment or pension is paid where the life insured is unlikely to ever follow any occupation for which they are reasonably qualified by education, training or experience. An Any Occupation policy can be funded from your personal bank account or superannuation fund.

- **Home Duties** – where a life insured is not able to perform any normal domestic duties or be engaged in any occupation for which they are reasonably qualified by training, education or experience. This can be funded from your personal bank account or superannuation fund.

Critical illness

A critical-illness policy is a lump sum that is paid to you in the event of a medical emergency or severe illness. The most common form of claim on this policy is due to cancer, heart attack, stroke or a motor-neuron-related disease. The insurance covers out-of-pocket medical expenses, rehabilitation expenses and costs of ongoing nursing care.

The premiums are not tax deductible and can only be paid from a personal bank account; your superannuation account cannot pay for trauma premiums. A critical-illness policy is also available to children.

Income protection

Your ability to earn an income is your greatest asset. An income protection policy caters for a percentage of your insured income if you become unable to work for an extended period of time.

Your income protection policy is tax deductible, so it can be held inside your superannuation fund or in your personal name. Unless you are constrained by cash flows, it is advisable that the policy is held in your own name to obtain a greater tax benefit and so that you do not have to meet a condition of release from your super fund in the event of a claim.

The features that are usually considered by an advisor are a policy's waiting period (thirty days, ninety days, two years), amount insured, occupation and benefit period (usually to age sixty-five, but it can vary).

Insurance and the role of your advisor

It's important to consider the amount of insurance that is necessary to your situation. For a family with young children and debts, all forms of insurance are absolutely essential. As you age and your liabilities are paid off, the risk of illness could compromise your retirement savings.

Table 3.1: Insurance for different life stages

Life stage	Life Insurance	Total Permanent Disablement	Critical Illness	Income Protection
Single, no dependants	✗		✓	✓
Married couple with a young family and mortgage	✓		✓	✓
Middle-aged couple with family, moderate debts, perhaps debt used to fund investment	✓		✓	✓
Empty nest, close to retirement	✗		✓	TBC

Your advisor will be able to help you determine an amount of cover that is in line with your budget and demonstrate the impact on your superannuation balance.

Insurance isn't homogenous. Different insurers will have different underwriting procedures and claims processes and will vary their assessment of medical conditions. As a result, the probability of claim and cost of the premium will vary, determined by the total amount of risk to the insurer.

Insurance can be complex, but your advisor will be able to 'go into the market' and have conversations with underwriters up front. When brokering an insurance policy on behalf of a client, they can ensure that it is tailored to the client's personal circumstances and health history.

REBECCA'S STORY – PART 1

Rebecca was introduced to me through a mortgage broker; she had recently been divorced from her husband of thirteen years. While there are always two sides to a story, the divorce was acrimonious to say the least. Rebecca's ex-husband was a chronic gambler and would quite often withdraw money from their joint account to fund his habits.

Rebecca was the sole proprietor of a payroll business. Her days were spent dealing with subcontractors and builders, people who were always chasing her to be paid. Money and finance came in, and then went out just as quickly.

Rebecca was exhausted. She had finally settled her divorce and was looking to move on and start afresh. While a new chapter in her life brought renewed optimism, it also brought inherited obligations. Rebecca now had sole custody of the couple's child, who was eleven years old and living with Asperger's.

Our session together was fun. Instead of getting together in an office, we met for cheese and chardonnay! As an independent mum with a business to run, she couldn't see any point in wasting any more time and energy. We talked about Rebecca's goals for the future and turned it into a game. She wanted a holiday and was in desperate need of one.

We put together a savings target for every three months and six months. Then we allocated a couple of weeks in each three-month period for her to chill out and give herself some space.

Now that Rebecca was running a business as a financially independent person, we talked about ways we could plan for the worst. It was Rebecca's desire to build a home and provide the best care for her son, and most of all, make sure he was protected against anything unforeseen. She wanted to ensure that, in the event of her passing, he could be taken care of without the influence of her ex-husband.

We came to the agreed insured amounts in Table 3.2 below.

Business insurance

A life and/or TPD insurance policy can be provided to an insured business owner. In the event of a claim, the proceeds can be administered to the shareholder's estate and their share in the company can be transferred to the remaining shareholder(s). If you're a business owner, it is prudent to manage your stakeholders and install responsible corporate governance. Whether it be a small- or medium-sized business, you need to install a succession plan in the event of ill health or the passing of a director or shareholder.

Table 3.2: Rebecca's insurance profile

	Life	TPD	Critical Illness	Income Protection
Mortgage	$500,000	$500,000	0	80% of gross package (including super-annuation payments)
Education expenses	$100,000	$100,000	0	
Cost of living				
Salary replacement			$280,000[22]	
Less super balance	$140,000	$140,000		
Insurance required	$460,000	$460,000	$200,000	$7,500/ month, 90-day wait, to age 65

In the best interests of shareholders, it is of the utmost importance to mitigate any risks to a key person in a company, especially any risks to the performance, wellbeing or profitability of that company and its stakeholders.

Buy/sell arrangements

The first consideration of insurance is the buy and sell arrangements. If one business owner was to pass away

---

22 We discussed cover as an indicative figure to account for any loss in business revenue and medical expenses. Any residual sums could contribute to a deposit for a home or mortgage. Critical illness amounts can vary depending on each individual situation.

or become incapacitated, what would the implications be for the other partner(s) or shareholders of this business? An insurance policy can address the value of the shareholder's stake in the company and its respective valuation.

It's worth discussing these insurance premiums with your advisor, as the structuring of the policies can be difficult and have significant implications if they are mishandled. Another issue to discuss is the arrangement for bringing on new shareholders to the business at some point in the future.

Considerations of ownership of the policies are:

- Self-owned

- Cross-owned

- Bare trust (in the event of bringing on future shareholders)

- Superannuation (rarely advised)

- Company (not advised)

In lieu of having a buy/sell arrangement put in place, it is worth consulting with your lawyer and having your company properly valued. This process requires time and financial commitment as there are many moving parts and complexities involved in drafting shareholders' agreements, a company valuation and an update to wills and powers of attorney.

Key person insurance

A key person of a company is one who has a large responsibility and/or generates a large amount of revenue for the business. If something were to happen to that person, such as an untimely death or incapacity, or if they were to become sick and unable to generate revenue, there could be consequences to the survivability of that business.

The premiums for this could be structured as either for capital purposes or for revenue purposes. Capital purposes may include extinguishing debt on a balance sheet or providing a lump sum to hire a new person. The premiums for this are not tax deductible. If the premium were for revenue purposes, this may add to the sum of replacing revenue that would ordinarily be generated by the key person. These premiums are tax deductible.

Planning your estate

Your estate represents your wishes and values, as well as how you will be remembered. For most people, the crucial estate planning document is a will. Approximately 50% of all Australians pass away without a will and have the estate administered by intestacy.

If you were to pass intestate, you face these risks:

- A legal precedent distributes assets

- Unnecessary and avoidable tax consequences

- Higher than expected time and costs to administer the estate

- Your estate may be left open to dispute

A financial advisor will collaborate with a solicitor on your estate planning objectives. Both advisor and law-yer will have an understanding of the tax benefits and consequences of the transfer of wealth. You can expect your advisor to make recommendations around a strategy and your solicitor to make sure that every-thing is watertight, checked off and will be executed correctly.

These conversations are never neutral. Confronting our mortality can be daunting. In an estate plan, con-sider:

- Making sure your assets are passed on according to your wishes

- Minimising the tax payable

- Making sure any gifts or donations are a reflection of your legacy

- Ensuring that you have an appropriate trustee in mind

- Distributing income for your family

- Taking the circumstances of your beneficiaries into consideration (special needs?)

- Appointing powers of attorney and guardians for any children

Estate assets

Companies and other assets that form a part of your estate are usually held in your personal name. How these assets will be allocated is determined by your will. The last thing that anyone wants is for their assets to be erroneously administered or their beneficiaries to have to go through intestacy, where the Supreme Court determines how a will is to be allocated. You can implement certain measures to prevent this, in conjunction with your financial advisor.

Testamentary trust

A trust is established by the will-maker and comes into effect upon that person's passing. It is an effective estate planning tool, particularly when the trustee has discretion and flexibility on how the income and assets will be distributed to the entitled beneficiaries.

The advantages of a testamentary trust are:

- Children are not subjected to minors' tax rates / penalty rates

- Protection from insolvency and other liabilities

- Capital gains tax (CGT) opportunities

- Protection from spendthrift beneficiaries (spouses)

Special disabilities trust

The purpose of a special disability trust must be to meet the reasonable care and accommodation needs of the beneficiary.

Superannuation – non-estate assets

These are assets that do not automatically form part of your estate and include your superannuation fund. It is important to consider how benefits will be paid according to your wishes in the event of your passing.

Options for nominations on your super fund:

- A binding nomination is where you nominate your beneficiaries in advance and the trustee of the superannuation fund must pay to a valid beneficiary.

- A non-binding nomination is where the trustee has discretion around who to pay the funds to.

- A reversionary beneficiary is where the pension reverts to a surviving spouse.

It is worth consulting which type of beneficiaries are applicable to you and drafting a strategy in lieu of any insurances with your financial advisor.

REBECCA'S STORY – PART 2

One of the significant features of Rebecca's situation was that she was operating her own business. If she was to pass away, the company would continue. Any debts associated with that business could be claimed on her estate, and therefore compromise her child.

Rebecca's solicitor was a great listener. Together, they drafted a will, powers of attorney and guardianship that covered all the bases, so that in a worst-case scenario, Rebecca's child could have the best shot at his welfare and happiness remaining protected.

Rebecca's superannuation fund strategy was to leave half the proceeds to the will and powers of attorney, while the remaining funds could establish an account-based pension for the benefit of the child.

The Tao of insurance and estate planning

Our time on this earth is finite and limited. Death is a part of life. As human beings, we crave order and certainty, but often live in denial about the fundamentally uncertain nature of life.

In our passing, our bodies are no longer burning calories to sustain our temperature and modus operandi. Our elements when cremated are released and radiate into space; our bodies when buried are transformed into matter, and so the circle of life continues. We fear death because we only know life. With that said, the knowledge that one day we will die brings focus to what it means to be alive and pushes us to express what we need to express: love.

This is the essence of establishing a will and taking out life insurance. The bequest in writing is a reflection of our love for the people we care most about that transcends space and time.

Summary

An insurance policy is a forward-looking contract where you pay a premium to protect yourself financially on an individual or business level against an insured event. The purpose of an estate plan is to ensure that your wishes and wealth are transferred to your beneficiaries without any fuss. In the event of an emergency or premature passing, it's important that you and/or your loved ones remain in a position where you're still money smart, can focus on what's essential and have the opportunity to live according to your values.

As we've discussed in this chapter, there are many kinds of insurance available to you and many ways to structure your estate. An advisor can be invaluable in determining the correct amount of insurance that pertains to your goals and objectives; they will devise a strategy on your behalf, understand all the bells and whistles of an insurance policy and show you the trade-off on your cash flow or superannuation balance.

Life is full of beautiful, positive moments, but it also throws up many unexpected challenges. Navigating life's highs and lows is not easy, mainly because we never know what's around the corner. That said, it is possible to minimise the risk of something unforeseen derailing our way of life.

If you would like to know more, download a copy of the Insurance and Estate Planning brochure in the resources page at www.equanimityfs.com.au/resources.

PART TWO
SUPERANNUATION

4
Understanding Super

The long-term trajectory of a person's financial journey is easy to track and predict. To achieve financial success, you need to prepare for retirement, the sooner, the better. While at various points in time, your financial goals will vary according to your current situation, the aim is for every individual to become a self-funded retiree.

In this chapter, we'll look at what superannuation is and the many benefits of investing in your super. We'll examine planning for retirement and the different ways that you can contribute to your super fund. We'll explore how superannuation works once you actually have retired, as well as taking a detailed look at a couple of real-life case studies. Finally, in the Tao of superannuation, we'll consider how you can ensure your super decisions reflect your core values.

What is superannuation?

Superannuation is a forced saving mechanism for the sole purpose of funding an income stream for your eventual retirement or, in the event of your death, for the benefits to be paid to your dependant(s) or legal representative. It was created as a means to offset the age pension and the merit of your super balance is defined by your contribution(s).

Superannuation is the tax-optimal place to invest (outside your family home), but there are stringent rules surrounding accessing funds. While it may be some time before you retire, your superannuation fund is still your money; it would be foolish to forget about it, as eventually you're going to need it.

How much will you need in retirement?

As a rule of thumb, your usual cost of living will reduce to two-thirds of your current expenditure when you retire. Keep in mind that your hobbies, car expenses, utility bills, healthcare, planned holidays, entertainment preferences and where you choose to live will ultimately determine how much you need. Your retirement usually starts at sixty-five. Assuming you are married, there is a chance that at least one of you will live to be 100.

The Association of Superannuation Funds of Australia retirement standards state that a modest retirement income for a couple is $62,269 per annum, but this may not be a suitable reflection of your desired lifestyle. In fact, I feel that number is a little light. To enjoy more holidays in retirement, say quarterly adventures, and a comfortable lifestyle, you'll probably need closer to $80,000 per annum. Keep in mind that the first ten years in retirement are usually the most expensive while you have great health, vitality and energy.

MY CALCULATIONS

As part of my service offering, I wanted to track what I could do for my clients so they could retire on their own terms, not somebody else's, nor be reliant on the age pension. I compared the median superannuation balance (over time from age 20 to 100) from the Australian census data of 2016 for a couple and mapped it according to a figure that excluded the value of a primary residence.

How much capital would a couple require to last them from age 65 to 100? At an assumed real interest rate of return of 4.5%, I came to the conclusion that you would require a sum close to $1.6 million, assuming you would live in your family home, leave your dependants an inheritance and not rely on the age pension.

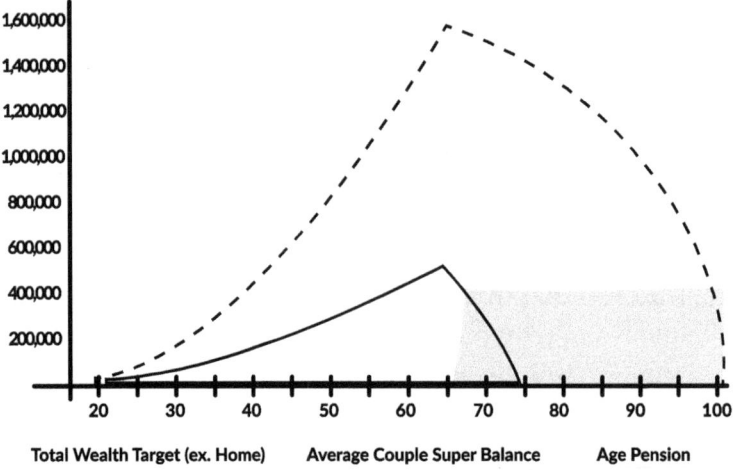

Total Wealth Target (ex. Home)   Average Couple Super Balance   Age Pension

Ultimately, this trajectory is something to keep in mind when putting your finances into perspective, irrespective of your life stage.

Investing in your super fund

There are two phases in superannuation, the first being accumulation mode, when you are contributing funds for retirement, the other being 'draw-down', where you are drawing funds that pay you an income once you have met a 'condition of release'.

Table 4.1: Tax advantages of investing in super

	Accumulation	Draw-down / account-based pension
Tax rate	15% on all concessional contributions and earnings	Zero
Capital gains	Greater than twelve months = discount by one-third (10%)	Zero
	Fewer than twelve months = no discount (15%)	
Minimum payments	9.50% super guarantee (SG) from employer (guaranteed contributions will progressively increase from 1 July 2021 and be capped at 12% by 1 July 2025)	Minimum pension payments (withdrawals) start at 4% and are increased per age bracket

Contributing to superannuation may attract tax deductions, offsets or even a government co-contribution.

Time

The long-term horizon is why your superannuation is imperative to growing your wealth. A golden rule when it comes to investing is that time and patience are your best friends. The longer your investment term, the longer your gains compound.

According to the behavioural economist Dan Ariely, 'Ultimately, people procrastinate and have a hard time understanding the real cost of not saving as well as

THE TAO OF WEALTH AND PROSPERITY

the benefits of saving.'[23] Consider this illustration and compare the portfolios:

Table 4.2: Accumulation of super funds over time

Assumptions	Portfolio A	Portfolio B
Initial balance	$10,000	$30,000
Payments per annum from employer	$1,200	$1,500
Number of years	45	35
Average return	9%	9%
Total at retirement	$1,114,303.34	$935,985.17

The person investing in portfolio A starts with a much smaller balance compared to the person investing in portfolio B, who is also receiving a higher payment each year from their employer. Yet portfolio A comes out on top.

Time invested, irrespective of market conditions, will always be your best friend. Ultimately, the person who is patient wins. By not accessing your super and utilising its structure at an early age, you will exponentially increase your wealth. In other words, the earlier you start and the more consistent you are with your contributions, the better off you will become.

---

23   D Ariely, *Predictably Irrational: The hidden forces that shape our decisions* (Harper Collins, Croydon, 2009), p241

Table 4.3: Last eight years' returns

Year	Portfolio A	Year	Portfolio B
37	$552,589.49	27	$461,437.17
45	$1,114,303.34	35	$935,985.17
Last 8 years' return	$561,713.85	Last 8 years' return	$474,548

It is worth noting that in both portfolios, the last eight years yielded the biggest gains, and the gains more than doubled during that period.

Drawbacks of investing inside your super fund

Once you make a contribution to your superannuation fund, you are only allowed to access the money once you have met a condition of release. The most common condition of release is when you reach the preservation age and decide to cease work/retire.

Table 4.4: Individual's preservation age for date of birth

Date of birth	Preservation age
Before 1 July 1960	55
1 July 1960–30 June 1961	56
1 July 1961–30 June 1962	57
1 July 1962–30 June 1963	58
1 July 1963–30 June 1964	59
From 1 July 1964	60

The main conditions of release are:

- Reaching preservation age and retiring

- Reaching preservation age and commencing a transition-to-retirement income stream (where you can draw a minimum of 4% of your balance, capped at a maximum withdrawal of 10%)

- Ceasing employment on or after age sixty

- Turning sixty-five (even if you haven't retired)

- Severe financial hardship

- Compassionate grounds

- Terminal illness

- Temporary or permanent incapacity

- Departing Australia (for certain visa holders)

- Death

In each of these situations and scenarios, there are tax consequences. Please seek professional advice.

Planning for retirement

Planning the right moment to retire can be one of the most difficult decisions of your life. This is the point when your human capital is exchanged for a sum of money which is expected to last until the end of your life. In my experience, the significance of this change is associated with a high degree of uncertainty for most people, including financial anxiety and, in some cases, a change of identity.

Australians are living longer and changes in healthcare and medicine are emphasising the need for flexibility to ensure your retirement income can fund newfound hobbies, holidays, your health and time you spend with family which will last well into your golden years.

Contributing to your superannuation fund

Concessional contributions. A concessional contribution is 'before tax'. In these cases, you or your employer can claim a tax deduction. A concessional contribution will form part of the taxable component of your superannuation fund. It is currently capped at $25,000 per annum and includes these types of contributions:

- Super guarantee

- Personal deduction

- Salary sacrifice

These contributions will incur an immediate 15% tax upon entry unless you are earning more than $250,000, for which you will pay 30% (Division 293 tax).

Non-concessional contributions and the bring-forward rule. A non-concessional contribution is money that is paid to your super fund 'after tax'. For this, you are not eligible to claim a tax deduction on the transfer. A non-concessional contribution will form part of the tax-free component of your superannuation fund.

Up until you are sixty-five, you can contribute $100,000 per annum to your super fund or trigger the bring-forward contribution, where you can make three years' worth of contributions ($300,000) at once. The drawback with the bring-forward rule is that you are not able to make any further contributions for the next three years.

When you're approaching retirement, it is advisable to make sure that any non-concessional contributions are made to a separate superannuation account so that the taxable and tax-free components are quarantined. Once you have established an account-based pension, you can draw from the taxable component of your retirement savings and mitigate the tax consequences to the estate.

When you're aged sixty-seven or over, you must meet the work test to make any further non-concessional contributions. You must have worked forty hours in a thirty-day period in a financial year. If you have met this test, the maximum non-concessional contribution you can make is $100,000 and the bring-forward rule can't be applied.

Small business concessions. When selling a small business and planning to retire, you may be eligible for certain concessions. These are best planned in conjunction with a tax expert and your accountant who can assist in administering the claim. The concessions that may be available to you are:

- The fifteen-year asset exemption
- The 50% active asset exemption
- The small business retirement exemption
- The small business asset rollover

All of these tests can be applied in an order that is designed to minimise your CGT and invest funds for your retirement.

Transfer balance cap

From 1 July 2017, the federal government imposed a cap on the amount of funds you are able to hold as an account-based pension. A limit of $1.6 million was applied per person to the funds you can hold in retirement/the draw-down phase.

NICK AND BRITTNEY'S STORY – PART 1

Nick (fifty-three) and Brittney (fifty-one) owned a medical centre, which they wanted to sell so they could retire. Nick and Brittney considered themselves fortunate and were proud to have served their community. The last of their six children had just finished school, and having flitted between packing

Table 4.5: Balance sheet before advice

	Assets			Liabilities	
Investment	Owner	Amount	Debt	Owner	Amount
Home	Joint	$1,200,000	Mortgage	Joint	$150,000
Shares	Family Trust	$1,220,000			
Cash	Family Trust	$80,000			
Business	Family Trust	$1,000,000			
Super	Nick	$1,200,000			
Super	Brittney	$1,100,000			$150,000
		$5,800,000	Net worth		$5,650,000

lunches and running a business for thirteen years, they felt it was time for a sea change.

A medical company was in the market, acquiring practices, and it had made them an offer to purchase their business for $1,000,000. There was a large amount of complexity with the sale going through, which added to the stress of their situation. Nick and Brittney also had assets held in a family trust with their children.

Both Nick and Brittney wanted to minimise their tax as much as possible, while retiring on $100,000 per annum, which they believed sufficient to have an overseas holiday every second year and maintain their current lifestyle. They were asked to stay working with the business for a period of twelve months to ensure any goodwill with the existing clients.

Table 4.6: Income and taxes breakdown before advice (tax rates at 2019/20 financial year)

	Nick	Brittney	Total
Base salary	$110,000	$75,000	$185,000
Interest	$0	$2,000	$2,000
Dividends (100% franked)	$50,000	$48,800	$98,800
Personal deductible contribution	$0.00	($17,875)	($17,875)
Taxable income	**$160,000**	**$107,925**	**$267,925**
Tax on income	($49,904)	($29,050)	($78,954)
Medicare levy	($3,200)	($2,159)	($5,359)
Franking credits (offset)	$21,429	$20,914	$42,343
Total tax payable	$31,675	$10,295	$41,970
Net income	**$128,325**	**$97,630**	**$225,955**

Given that the majority of their assets were to be
structured inside superannuation, there was a chance
that they would eventually surpass the transfer balance
cap. They needed funds to get them across the line to
extinguish their loan and supplement their cost of living
once they stopped working, as they couldn't access
any money from their superannuation until they turned
sixty. Given that they had also sold the business, they
would be receiving a lesser salary and no dividends from
the company.

The advice was incredibly complex. As it involved a lot
of moving parts, it had to draw from a lot of different
strategies and tax calculations. Nick and Brittney's
reputation also had to be taken into consideration.

The first phase of the strategy was to identify which
small business contributions would apply and how we
could minimise their capital gain footprint. In this case,
I worked alongside Nick and Brittney's accountant, who
had confirmed that the 50% active asset exemption and
the small business retirement exemption applied.

Table 4.7: Tax exemptions

Sale		$1,000,000.00
CGT discount	50%	$500,000.00
50% active asset test reduction	50%	$250,000.00
Retirement exemption		$250,000.00

It turned out that Nick and Brittney's assessable capital
gains were only $250,000 to be split among all eight
beneficiaries of their family trust, so the clients had to

pay only a minimal amount of tax from the sale of their business.

In retirement

Re-contribution

A re-contribution strategy is where you have met a condition of release and make a withdrawal from your superannuation fund, then recontribute the monies as a non-concessional contribution. The purpose of this is to 'cleanse' the taxable component of your superannuation account and increase the tax-free component. The benefit is that it reduces the amount of tax payable to a 'SIS' – Superannuation Industry (Supervision) Act 1993 – dependant when the member passes (see next chapter for tax consequences on the estate).

Account-based pension

An account-based pension is established once you have met a condition of release, usually when you retire. A feature of an account-based pension is that you pay no tax on earnings or capital gains. You must make a minimum payment each financial year, corresponding to your age bracket as shown in Table 4.8.

THE TAO OF WEALTH AND PROSPERITY

Table 4.8: Minimum payments for account-based pensions

Age	Minimum withdrawal	Reduced rates by 50% for the 2019–20 and 2020–21 income years (COVID)
Under 65	4.0%	2.0%
65–74	5.0%	2.5%
75–79	6.0%	3.0%
80–84	7.0%	3.5%
85–89	9.0%	4.5%
90–94	11.0%	5.5%
95 or over	14.0%	7.0%

NICK AND BRITTNEY'S STORY – PART 2

Now that they had decided to retire, Nick and Brittney were stumped as to what they were going to do with their sea change. They had been busy running a household and living in a tightknit family. Some of their children had finished university and were leaving the nest, Brittney's father had recently passed away and Nick was unsure what post-work would look like.

Everyone was in good health, finances weren't a problem, but spiritually and emotionally, both Nick and Brittney were exhausted and anxious about how they were going to spend their time and energy. In the privacy of their own time, Nick and Brittney considered what the future would look like. It wasn't a matter of restructuring their finances, but repurposing their welfare and livelihood.

Nick had been a keen surfer growing up while Brittney had always had a passion for the arts. In their own time, they came to the conclusion that living the city life was not for them, so they decided to sell the home and relocate to a coastal town an hour's drive from Sydney. The kids could still visit whenever they pleased, and financially, Mum and Dad would be there to lend a hand if need be.

This decision gave them both a purpose: planning the design of a new home. Nick loved project management while Brittney had a sharp eye for detail. They designed a dream home by the beach where they had their projects together as well as their own individual hobbies. Spiritually, though, there was still a void, so they decided to commit one day per fortnight to a local charity and serve on a phone helpline for people struggling with mental illness.

The next step in Nick and Brittney's plan was to determine how much they required to get them across the period between when they finished working and could officially retire. They wanted to maximise their superannuation, which involved restructuring their balance sheet. I developed detailed modelling over ten years so that they had an understanding of what the metrics could look like and how their cost of living would affect their capital. With the details all in black and white, Nick and Brittney found it much easier to move confidently into the future.

The Tao of superannuation

Let's dream for a second. If money wasn't a limitation, what would retirement look like to you? How are you going to spend your time? What are your recreational and lifestyle goals?

It's one thing to write down your goals, it's another to draw them. Start by creating a vision board of the places you would like to visit, languages you would like to learn, hobbies that are going to keep you busy. Does this visualisation look like days on the golf course, time spent with grandchildren, bridge clubs or caravanning around Australia? Will you relocate and downsize?

Retiring is something that should be fun. Like all experiences, it's best when shared with the people close to you – some things are worth more than 'just money'. How is your retirement going to maintain your sense of purpose and bring you fulfilment?

A vision board is useful to make dreams into something tangible. Don't hide it; make sure it's something everyone in your household can see and be proud of.

In the diagram below, I've listed seven things to consider for a fruitful retirement. Use it to help you find your central values when it comes to your transition out of work.

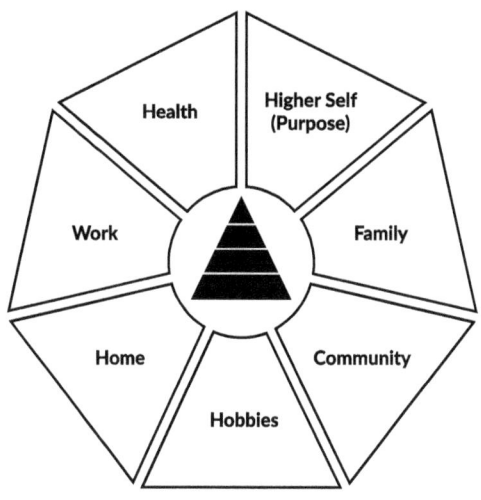

Summary

The sole purpose of superannuation is to fund your retirement and take the stress load off the age pension. The earlier you start investing in your superannuation, the better off you will be when you retire, and the government offers generous incentives for you to do just that.

When it comes to planning for retirement, there are many ways to structure your contributions to your super account, as well as your transition out of work, taking into account taxation and your estate. It pays to obtain advice from a financial planner who can model the complex scenarios of your different options.

Beyond the numbers, the most important aspect of your retirement planning is to ensure that this time in your life fulfils your higher goals, whether they are the arts, spending time with family, a spiritual calling, a sea change or serving your community. The moment of retirement is when all your chickens come home to roost. Where you stand will be a reflection of how you've utilised your super and invested throughout your life. Wherever that is, this time of life is about self-acceptance and being at peace with your decisions.

5
Choosing Your Superannuation Fund

Choosing a super fund that is relevant to your circumstances is one of the most important investment decisions you will make. It's essential to understand all the benefits and risks of your product. Think of your superannuation fund like a car: you can have the sleekest and sexiest design, but it's what's underneath the bonnet that truly counts.

The question is, with so many options out there, how do you make a choice? Would an industry super fund be a better option for you? Or perhaps a public-offer fund (aka a wrap platform) would meet your needs. And then there are self-managed superannuation funds (SMSFs) – what are the considerations for going out on your own?

In this chapter, we'll look at the different kinds of superannuation funds and the factors to take into consideration when choosing one.

Super FIT

When you're considering a super fund, it's important to check that it's 'super FIT' – that is, it's the right fit for fees, investments and tax implications. It's also important to check that it's fit for purpose in accordance with your life stage and financial objectives.

As part of the 5Cs (see Chapter 1), the step 'Calibrate' is designed to ensure that your financial products are fit for purpose. It's important to ensure that a super fund (or insurance product) is aligned to your primary goals and objectives and will mitigate any financial risks, which we'll discuss in later chapters.

A common mistake I see people make is chasing returns, paying attention to recent events in the media which promise superior returns on certain funds compared to the others. While this is an important consideration, usually these reports are only partially true, as product providers love to boast about being 'at the top end of town'.

Returns are influenced by a multiplicity of factors, such as the size of funds under management (FUM), age of members, as well as their demographics and occupations, the trustee's investment mandate, seasonality of returns, the length of establishment of the fund, timing of underlying investments being purchased and the flow of monies being drawn down by members. Today there is so much data available that tracking returns becomes a cesspool of statistics. They can be very difficult to compare and open to interpretation.

Different products are suitable for different people. It wouldn't be fair if your grandmother tried to four-wheel drive in the bush in her Skyline alongside a fully kitted Land Rover – her vehicle is just not fit for purpose. Ultimately, the choice of your superannuation fund comes down to you.

Let's take a look at what's underneath the bonnet and uncover all the benefits and risks of each type of fund.

Public sector funds

In the past, employees of state, territory and Commonwealth governments had to be members of public sector funds. Many public servants now have a choice of super fund, particularly if they are employed outside core government departments.

Payments from public sector funds can come in the form of a defined benefit at retirement which pays you a guaranteed income stream. They are supported by their own actuaries and investment committees to ensure that the funds invested are designed to meet all payments until the member's and/or spouse's passing. In the event of failure, these funds are usually guaranteed by the taxpayer.

Industry funds

Initially, industry funds were set up to service the superannuation needs of specific industries such as health, hospitality and construction. Over time, there have been mergers and transfers that have reduced the number and created giant funds for employees in many industries. Increasingly, industry funds are permitting members of the public to join, thus providing this market with an alternative to retail funds.

The main advantage of industry superannuation funds is their lower fee structures. Who should choose an industry fund? According to APRA's annual fund-level superannuation statistics (June 2019, published 10 December 2019),[24] as an indicative guide, 60% of members in industry superannuation funds are aged under fifty-four. These funds predominately have a younger client base who will be contributing to their superannuation accounts for a long period of time. As a result, these funds have the ability to operate at scale.

---

24 'Annual fund-level superannuation statistics' (APRA, 2020), www.apra.gov.au/annual-fund-level-superannuation-statistics, accessed 14 January 2021

Industry funds quite often have default/diversi-fied investment options and a small number of other investment choices in a pool known as a unit trust. The superannuation account holder owns units in this investment option, which is pooled with all other members of the fund. These funds also have exposure to private equity, unlisted assets and venture capital, which most people could not otherwise access.

Industry funds are great for people who have lower balances, are young, have a relatively simple finan-cial situation and have a long horizon to invest. This group of people can take advantage of market volatil-ity and withstand any share-market corrections.

Industry funds do have their drawbacks. Because of their unit-trust structure, there is little visibility over investments that are entirely under the control of the fund manager. As a member, you merely own units in the trust and do not have any control of the underly-ing assets of the fund. While industry funds do pub-lish their investment mandates and have governance around the valuations of their underlying assets, investors are still subject to the discretion of the fund manager and their defined asset allocation.

This can prove problematic, in particular, for clients who are looking to retire within a ten-year period, as they could be subject to an investment mandate that is not in line with the amount of risk they are willing to take in the event of a correction. Notable examples of this happened during the Global Financial Crash (GFC) and more recently in the COVID-19 market crash.

When investing in unlisted assets, investors in a unit trust can be caught off guard in the event of a liquidity trap, when units of the trust are frozen by the fund manager. This happens when everyone wants to withdraw from a fund at the same time and the fund manager does not have the time or capacity to sell the underlying asset. When this happened during the GFC, a number of investors were caught out.

When you're considering an industry super fund, it is worth noting how it is marketed to the general public in comparison to industry benchmarks. For instance, as it stands now, Australian Super has a standard default option labelled as a 'Balanced Default', with approximately 70% of funds invested in growth assets (a 70/30 split). If you compare this to the industry benchmark used by Morningstar, the balanced option contains a 50/50 split of growth to defensive mix.[25]

To the naked eye, this could be an inaccurate reflection of a 'balanced' strategy when someone is comparing returns between a benchmark and comparable fund. It is worth noting that the returns published periodi-

---

25 Information based on an AustralianSuper Product Disclosure Statement dated 1 April 2020 and Investment Guide dated June 2019 – see 'AustralianSuper product disclosure statements' (Australian-Super, no date), www.australiansuper.com/tools-and-advice/learn/product-disclosure-statements, accessed 14 January 2021

cally are based on the performance of the fund, not a member's portfolio.

With that said, given the valuations and exposure to private equity, investors closer to retirement may want to consider placing an emphasis on quality stocks and liquidity to prevent any significant fluctuations in their account balance, and choose a superannuation fund with more transparency in the underlying assets and more flexibility to manage their portfolio. Depending on your financial situation and the complexity of your circumstances, it's worth thoroughly investigating if an industry fund is relevant to your needs, as you could be exposed to unnecessary risks otherwise.

Public-offer funds: wrap platform

A public-offer or retail fund is one that is regulated by APRA and made available for commercial purposes. These superannuation funds usually have an aligned distribution network with financial advisors and have previously been retailed through larger financial services companies.

These types of superannuation funds come in the form of a wrap platform – where the member owns the underlying units of each investment option. What sets a wrap platform apart is its transparency, wider range of investments and flexibility: you are able to access direct equities listed on the Australian share market and international markets, term deposits, cash account and a suite of managed funds and separately managed accounts. Given the freedom of choice available in a wrap platform, a client may be eligible to achieve greater performance or risk-adjusted returns, overseen by an advisor, compared to other types of superannuation funds in the market.

Another feature of these types of platforms is that you are able to track your individual portfolio and review its performance over a period of your choice. The advantage to holding a wrap platform is that the portfolio, performance and adjustments can be customised to your preferences and individual circumstances. Wrap platforms aren't confined in singularity to superannuation, but can also be owned as an investment account by an individual, company, family trust or SMSF.

Traditionally, due to distribution networks being aligned with the banks, there was a push to price wrap platforms so that they could be bundled together with a commercial benefit that favoured the retailer. In addition, the technology was cumbersome and the default investment options were quite often expensive and underperformed according to a benchmark. In recent times, advances in technology and increased competition in wrap platforms have brought the pricing down considerably, making them more favourable to the consumer.

When I am giving financial advice, I am platform agnostic and endeavour to recommend the platform that is best suited to the investment strategy of my client. A wrap platform is usually priced marginally higher than an industry fund, which warrants a conversation about my client's long-term objective. It is imperative that you can align and justify the fees with your personal goals so that you are aware of the benefits and mitigate any risks.

Self-managed superannuation funds

SMSFs have come under increasing scrutiny by the regulator, whose research found that 'SMSFs are not suitable for members with a low fund balance, particularly where they have limited ability to make future contributions. This is important because consumers starting off with a low balance need to be aware that they may not be in a better financial position in the future by holding an SMSF compared with investing in an APRA-regulated fund'.[26]

As determined by the Australian Securities and Investment Committee (ASIC), from 1 July 2016, SMSF advice can be provided only by an advisor who is authorised, adequately trained and holds the correct qualifications. It is the advisor's responsibility to open

---

26   G Colley 'Shots fired: ASIC raises red flags on SMSFs' (AMP Capital, The SMSF Suite, 17 October 2019), www.ampcapital.com/au/en/ insights-hub/articles/2019/october/shots-fired-asic-raises-red-flags-on-smsfs, accessed 14 January 2021

up and establish a dialogue about whether an SMSF is fit for purpose, and the advisor has a duty of care to their client. The exemption to accountants from certain requirements in relation to the establishment of an SMSF ceased on 30 June 2016. By law, and under the heading of the safe harbour provisions, an advisor must review the trustee (individual or corporate) and the suitability of the fund on an annual basis as the fees and responsibility of the trustees must be validated.

The advantage of having an SMSF is that it provides you with more flexibility and freedom to choose your investment strategy, particularly in direct property, unlisted shares and alternative assets. An SMSF also warrants greater responsibility compared to a retail (public-offer) or industry superannuation fund, because you are effectively both trustee and member. As trustee, you are ultimately making decisions for the members of your fund and the penalties can be significant if your SMSF were found to be non-compliant. It's best to consult with a financial advisor to determine whether an SMSF is suited to you, so that you don't incur the risk of being non-compliant. Your advisor and/or registered tax agent will be able to give you a clear answer about whether this kind of fund is suited to you.

It is of the utmost importance that you understand what to consider when establishing and administering an SMSF. In the end, the suitability of an SMSF comes down to you.

Drafting and executing an investment strategy

A common mistake occurs when all of a client's SMSF investments are held in cash or purely in one asset class. Diversification is key to a good investment strategy. Keep in mind that you're investing for your retirement nest egg, and the timeline of investing could be up to forty years.

Particularly with SMSFs, you can invest in niche asset classes such as unlisted shares, commercial property, debt instruments and certain alternative assets (direct commodities). Whatever your preference may be, you can have more freedom to choose these assets, should they be aligned with your investment preferences and objectives.

The Australian Tax Office (ATO) will take into consideration the risks of inadequate diversification within the context of your SMSF investment portfolio. The ATO will also consider whether making, holding and realising the likely return from your fund investments aligns with your retirement objectives and expected cash-flow requirements.

There is a cost to serving an SMSF, which may be an impediment on returns. Any excess fees that you pay are lost opportunities, as they could have been accumulating as savings over a long timeframe. SMSFs require time to operate and incur trustee obligations, as well as ASIC and accounting fees – all these costs must be taken into consideration. If an SMSF is holding its investments within an underlying investment wrap platform, it is merely operating in the same way as an ordinary public-offer fund or wrap platform. If this is the case, the client is better off avoiding the minimum $3,000 per annum in additional accounting fees and the unaccountable costs in time.

An SMSF may be suitable to sophisticated investors who are able to invest for their retirement because they have the time, expertise and ability to do so. The accounting fees can be justified as most of the trading can be undertaken directly from the fund's bank account and there is potential for cost savings in the absence of holding assets on an investment wrap platform owned by the SMSF.

Borrowing and making limited recourse arrangements

An SMSF is most suitable for people who want to borrow funds for investing, predominantly for the purchase of a commercial property, and where a small business (company) can pay rent into the SMSF. This is particularly beneficial for small business owners who essentially want to retain funds 'in the family' so that the rental payments can provide a steady source of income for the superannuation fund. With these arrangements, everything must be made at arm's length, ensuring the fund doesn't breach the in-house asset test. An in-house asset cannot be greater than 5% and is any of the following:

- A loan to or an investment in a related party of your fund

- An investment in a related trust of your fund

- An asset of your fund that is leased to a related party (with the notable exception of business real property)

It's important to be aware of the risks of this strategy. A business premises is usually a large asset and purchasing it ties up capital in the fund, which may preclude other investment opportunities, causing a lack of diversification. This might not match your risk profile.

As purchasing a property is a large single transaction, consider whether you are borrowing too much. If you are not in a position to make extra concessional or non-concessional contributions to your super fund, and the rent you'll earn is not sufficient to cover the loan repayments, the ATO may find your fund non-compliant due to a loss of revenue within the business.

Providing insurance

As a trustee of an SMSF, you are responsible for making sure that all members have been offered or have access to insurance. The biggest mistake people make is when they close their previous retail/industry fund and roll over the proceeds into a new SMSF without having any insurance in place. By closing your old superannuation fund, you lose any insurance that was attached to it.

The most common forms of insurance that are held inside superannuation are life and TPD, but income protection can also be included if necessary. The ATO will look at whether insurance cover should be held for one or more members.

Estate planning

As a trustee, you have the final say on what happens to assets – ie what is passed to who. The consequences of not having a binding nomination on the fund can be significant. It is worth addressing your estate and succession plan, particularly if you are running a small business in lieu of having an SMSF.

An increasing risk for Australians is the combination of longevity, age care and powers of attorney should someone suffer incapacity. If a complex situation arose in your family and you had significant assets held in superannuation, an SMSF may be suitable if you wish an independent third party to cater for your welfare and livelihood. For ease of management, an independent third party and power of attorney may be well situated to administer a person's superannuation savings and minimise the dealings with a public-offer or industry fund's team of administrators.

In this event, a situation may arise which could have significant tax consequences associated with the estate. In the event of a person's untimely death, the benefits of superannuation could be preserved. In this instance, a trustee can commute the taxable component of your retirement savings and recontribute it as a non-concessional. By cleansing the components, you reduce the amount of tax you pay in the form of an income stream or to the estate.

Strategies may be available to have superannuation assets transferred from an elderly member and recontributed to a younger member's superannuation balance – particularly in a situation where a family business is operating a commercial property owned by the SMSF. The total wealth of the family is succeeded in the optimal environment for mitigating any tax consequences at a later point in time.

Liquidity and control of underlying assets

Liquidity is always an important consideration when you're drafting an investment strategy. The last thing you want to do is paint yourself into a corner by holding 100% property or an unlisted asset that is difficult to sell.

The ATO will consider the liquidity of your investments, allowing the fund to meet costs and pay benefits (pension payments) when you retire. It is essential, particularly where an SMSF has large member balances (greater than $1.6 million per member as an estimated rule of thumb), that sufficient cash reserves are kept aside for various purposes such as smoothing investment returns, retaining assets in the fund and facilitating anti-detriment payments in relation to death benefits.

In terms of controlling the underlying assets, situations may arise where there is a reason to sell assets with a higher cost base or crystallise previous losses to mitigate a capital gain. You can still achieve this in an ordinary wrap platform, and you are able to pool assets with other members. This is particularly beneficial with members who hold large superannuation balances as you can take advantage of tax arbitrages where the assets have been segregated per member.

Reviewing the trustee structure

What structure will you choose? Individual or company? They have vastly different implications on succession planning and penalties for noncompliance.

Unbeknown to a lot of SMSF trustees, you must review the structure every year. This doesn't mean it has to be changed, but you must document that it has at least been addressed. SMSFs have recently come under increasing scrutiny by the regulator.

NICK AND BRITTNEY'S STORY – PART 3

Nick and Brittney needed someone to mentor and help them with their financial management and superannuation. They wanted to optimise their tax position and benefit their children in the best way possible. 'Once a mum, always a mum,' Brittney said, while Nick wanted their children to find their own path. Nick and Brittney were also making adjustments through handing over their business, working for twelve months, and then finding a new Zen.

Previously, the couple had their superannuation accounts with an industry superannuation fund. We discussed the benefits and the risks of each super fund and considered an SMSF as an option available to them. Their accountant had explained the benefits of utilising an SMSF to control assets' cost base and mitigate the super fund's capital gain arbitrage, but this meant both Nick and Brittney spending further time and energy concentrating on an SMSF in addition to administering the family trust, building a new home and enjoying time away from the family, plus the expense of accounting and ASIC fees.

Ultimately, all parties met in the middle and rolled the existing funds from an industry fund into two separate public-offer funds. It turned out to be cheaper and more effective in terms of time spent concentrating on administration and energy directed to running their accounts, which could have prevented them from enjoying their hobbies.

Nick and Brittney could now quarantine the super savings with the highest taxable component to run down funds for their children's pre-inheritance, which would go to fund a deposit on each child's home. This would preclude any tax paid on the estate should they both pass away and have superannuation funds paid to a SIS dependant.

Table 5.1: Nick and Brittney's case study (projections years 1 to 5)

	Year 1	Year 2	Year 3	Year 4	Year 5
Combined salaries	$140,000	$0	$0	$0	$0
Interest	$2,000	$2,000	$2,000	$2,000	$2,000
Dividends (fully franked)	$88,800	$76,800	$49,709	$42,962	$45,119
Pension income (Nick)	$0	$0	$0	$0	$0
Pension income (Brittney)	$0	$0	$0	$0	$0
FT distributions	$0	$38,286	$58,656	$70,746	$75,279
Gross income	**$230,800**	**$117,086**	**$128,696**	**$131,588**	**$130,663**
Concessional contributions Nick	($25,000)	($25,000)	($25,000)	($25,000)	($25,000)
Concessional contributions Brittney	($25,000)	($25,000)	($25,000)	($25,000)	($25,000)
Income tax	($23,622)	$0	$0	$0	$0
Franking credit refund	$38,057	$32,914	$21,304	$18,412	$19,337
Expenses	($100,000)	($100,000)	($100,000)	($100,000)	($100,000)
Gifting	$0	$0	$0	$0	$0
Surplus cash flow	**$95,235**	**$0**	**$0**	**$0**	**$0**

Continued

Table 5.1 cont.

	Year 1	Year 2	Year 3	Year 4	Year 5
Balance sheet					
Family trust					
Shares	$1,920,000	$1,701,000	$1,471,050	$1,334,603	$1,296,333
Cash	$80,000	$175,235	$80,000	$80,000	$80,000
Non-concessional contribution – Nick	($100,000)	($100,000)	($100,000)	-	-
Non-concessional contribution - Brittney	($100,000)	($100,000)	($100,000)	($100,000)	-
Withdrawals		-$38,286	-$58,656	-$70,746	-$75,279
Total assets (F/T)	**$1,800,000**	**$1,676,235**	**$1,351,050**	**$1,314,603**	**$1,376,333**
Superannuation					
Nick super 1	$1,225,000	$1,312,500	$1,404,375	$1,500,844	$1,602,136
Nick super 2	$100,000	$200,000	$300,000	$315,000	$330,750
Total super Nick	**$1,325,000**	**$1,512,500**	**$1,704,375**	**$1,815,844**	**$1,932,886**
Brittney super 1	$1,125,000	$1,151,250	$1,177,500	$1,203,750	$1,230,000
Brittney super 2	$100,000	$200,000	$300,000	$420,000	$441,000
Total super Brittney	**$1,225,000**	**$1,351,250**	**$1,477,500**	**$1,623,750**	**$1,671,000**
Total net worth	**$4,350,000**	**$4,539,985**	**$4,532,925**	**$4,754,197**	**$4,980,219**

Table 5.2: Nick and Brittney's case study (projections years 10 to 15)

	Year 10	Year 11	Year 12	Year 13	Year 14	Year 15
Combined salaries	$0	$0	$0	$0	$0	$0
Interest	$2,000	$2,000	$2,000	$2,000	$2,000	$2,000
Dividends (fully franked)	$36,672	$28,005	$18,906	$19,662	$20,448	$21,266
Pension income (Nick)#	$98,876	$101,366	$104,215	$107,812	$111,629	$115,602
Pension income (Brittney)#	$73,964	$73,139	$72,371	$71,662	$71,015	$70,434
FT distributions	$7,640	$2,599	$2,736	$3,190	$4,482	$4,354
Gross income	**$219,152**	**$207,110**	**$200,227**	**$204,326**	**$209,575**	**$213,655**
Concessional contribution Nick*	($25,000)	($25,000)	($25,000)	($25,000)	($25,000)	($25,000)
Concessional contribution Brittney*	($25,000)	($25,000)	($25,000)	($25,000)	($25,000)	($25,000)
Income tax	$0	$0	$0	$0	$0	$0
Expenses	($100,000)	($100,000)	($100,000)	($100,000)	($100,000)	($100,000)
Gifting	($84,956)	($69,101)	($58,313)	($47,418)	($51,851)	($55,623)

Continued

Table 5.2 cont.

	Year 10	Year 11	Year 12	Year 13	Year 14	Year 15
Surplus cash flow	$0	$0	$0	$0	$0	$0
Balance sheet						
Family trust assets						
Shares	$916,794	$700,134	$472,641	$491,547	$511,209	$531,657
Cash	$80,000	$80,000	$80,000	$80,000	$80,000	$80,000
Non-concessional contribution – Nick	$0	$0	$0	$0	$0	$0
Non-concessional contribution – Brittney	$0	$0	$0	$0	$0	$0
Withdrawals	($7,640)	($2,599)	($2,736)	($3,190)	($4,482)	($4,354)
Total family trust	**$989,154**	**$777,535**	**$549,905**	**$568,357**	**$586,727**	**$607,303**
Superannuation						
Nick super 1	$2,114,824	$2,171,816	$2,231,656	$2,294,489	$2,360,464	$2,429,737
Nick super 2	$422,130	$443,237	$465,398	$488,668	$513,102	$538,757
Withdrawals	($65,044)	($80,899)	($91,687)	($87,853)	($82,830)	($78,446)

Continued

Table 5.2 cont.

	Year 10	Year 11	Year 12	Year 13	Year 14	Year 15
Total super Nick	$2,471,910	$2,534,154	$2,605,367	$2,695,304	$2,790,736	$2,890,048
Brittney super 1	$1,286,250	$1,237,500	$1,188,750	$1,140,000	$1,091,250	$1,042,500
Brittney super 2	$562,840	$590,982	$620,531	$651,558	$684,136	$718,343
Total super Brittney	$1,849,090	$1,828,482	$1,809,281	$1,791,558	$1,775,386	$1,760,843
Total net worth	$5,310,154	$5,140,171	$4,964,553	$5,055,219	$5,152,849	$5,258,194

^ Deficit funded by commutation from Nick super account 1 and from surplus cash flows.

* For the purposes of this illustration, we have assumed no significant capital gains consequences and any personal income tax that could be liable has been offset by a concessional contribution.

All pension income is not assessable to Nick and Brittney's personal income tax.

It gave Nick and Brittney freedom to mitigate the cost base of any CGT arbitrage, which they could also house in an SMSF, and opened up opportunities to mitigate unforeseen tax consequences to the estate and help their children purchase their first homes.

Nick and Brittney had not yet reached the age when they could access their super. At that point, a self-managed superannuation fund could be reconsidered. (See Tables 5.1 and 5.2 above.)

Explanation of numbers: This modelling is a projection of cash flow, expenditure, gifting and contribution strategies. It is an indicative guide only and demonstrates how assets can be restructured from one entity to another in lieu of a client's personal cash flows, goals and objectives; the modelling demonstrates how balances can compound over time. A financial advisor will be able to demonstrate financial projections in a statement of advice.

The Tao of choosing a super fund

Superannuation is an area where consumers often do not have enough information about the products they are buying. It is vitally important for you to keep your own values in focus and get the financial advice you need so you can make an informed choice. Otherwise, you may fall prey to fashions, whims and asymmetries in the market. It's the role of an advisor, as a fiduciary, to disclose any conflicts of interest and make a recommendation on a super fund that is in the client's best interest.

'The market for "lemons"' by George Akerlof[27] is a great example of asymmetries in the market, but for all the wrong reasons. Akerlof looked at the market for new cars and used cars being sold by various dealer groups to consumers. What would happen to the integrity of the market if buyers could not differentiate between the high-quality new cars (peaches) and the low-quality used cars (lemons) and were only willing to pay a fixed price for a car without regard to its quality?

In any market, there is always an asymmetry of information. In this case, it was only the sellers in the car market who could distinguish between the peaches and the lemons. Because the buyers in the market were only willing to pay a fixed price, the lemons ended up dominating because they were cheaper. The demand for peaches evaporated and the market became flooded with lemons. Everybody lost.

The message here is that your super fund has to be fit for purpose and aligned to mitigate the risks of your current situation. Just because a certain type of superannuation fund is popular doesn't mean it's right for you. You must ensure your super choice enables you to achieve your objectives and that the fees you are paying can be justified. While it may be true that you can't access your super funds for a long time, it's still

---

27 GA Akerlof, 'The market for "lemons": Quality uncertainty and the market mechanism', *The Quarterly Journal of Economics*, 84:3 (August 1970), pp488–500

your money, so make sure it's managed according to your ideals. There's no point in structuring your super in a way that leaves you no time to live the life of your dreams.

Summary

When you're choosing a super fund, it's important to consider how far you are from retirement. Younger investors can take advantage of longer timeframes to ride out the inevitable market fluctuations associated with riskier investments, but if you're within ten years of retirement, it may pay to invest in more conservative areas. Also, watch out for the labels – one fund's 'balanced' investment may not be in line with your idea of balanced, or even industry benchmarks.

Although SMSFs represent one-third of the superannuation scene in Australia, and approximately one-third of all investments inside superannuation, they may not be fit for purpose for your personal situation. Advances in technology, the accessibility of financial instruments and the cost reductions of traditional public-offer super funds mean that an SMSF is only recommended in limited circumstances. In making this recommendation, the advisor has a responsibility to ensure that all avenues have been explored, as there are significant penalties for getting it wrong.

The best advice is to get advice! Find a financial advisor who you trust and who understands your values and priorities, so you can ensure your superannuation choices meet your needs.

PART THREE
TAX AND DEBT

6
The Taxman And The Publican

The reason we pay tax is to uphold the social fabric of our society. The success of our community depends on cooperation and an alignment of civic values. As part of the 5Cs, we *create* a financial plan that takes into account the tax consequences of investing and insurance, while minimising the amount of tax we pay.

In this chapter, we'll look at tax advice, and the difference between advice from your accountant or tax agent and advice from your financial advisor. We'll also look at when you need to pay tax, using the all-Aussie pub test. We'll explore the different kinds of tax (income and capital gains), the different ways to structure your finances and the tax implications of each one.

Minimising your tax and investing in the correct structure can help you reach your financial goals. When it comes to wealth creation, always go into an investment or strategy to make money first. Paying tax is important, but unlike your trusted local publican, the tax man doesn't deserve a tip!

The role of your financial advisor

It's important to focus on minimising your tax with appropriate strategies and deductions, not avoiding it. There are various types of taxes, with different ones applying to income and capital. Different investment entities have different tax rates, benefits and implications.

Your accountant or a registered tax agent is the expert in this field. Most of the time, financial advisors are not tax experts per se and won't be able to implement or fulfil the role of your accountant. Financial advisors do, however, have a good grasp of tax law and how to engineer a strategy which takes into account the goal of minimising your tax footprint. And taxation warrants consideration – if you do end up paying more in tax, it is hopefully because you have made more money!

Does it pass the pub test?

Australians live and die by the principle of giving everyone a fair go. Paying tax does have its advantages: it enables public and social utilities for the benefit of everyone and prevents crime, but as an individual, you are allowed and entitled to minimise the amount of tax you pay. After all, it is still money that you have earned.

How do you know what's fair? Tax law is complicated, and for most of us even the basics are overwhelming. But we can all apply one simple rule to defining our tax obligations by asking, 'Does it pass the pub test?'

Are you in the pub?

We love the pub in Australia. It seems to be ingrained in our DNA: our glorified little casinos filled with poker machines, a TAB, chicken parmies, bourbon-n-cokes and overpriced beer – only in Australia!

It may sound obvious, but it is essential for tax purposes to know if you are in or out of the pub, so the first thing you must do is to determine whether you are a resident or non-resident of Australia. A person is a resident of Australia if they pass any one of the following four tests:

- They reside in Australia
- Their domicile is Australia, which applies unless the ATO is satisfied that the person's permanent place of abode is outside of Australia

- They are in Australia for at least 183 days in a year of income, unless it can be established that the person's usual place of abode is outside Australia

- They are a contributing member of a superannuation fund for Commonwealth government officers

Identification, please!

Children under the age of eighteen are subject to special tax rates. Under these rates, minors have a tax-free threshold of $416 on eligible income, but 'excepted income' derived by minors is taxed at marginal adult rates. This excepted income includes that gained from employment, inherited assets and testamentary trust allocations.

Is it a fair go?

Are you bloody taking the piss, mate? There is a distinction between avoiding and minimising tax. Part IVA of the Income Tax Assessment Act (1936) deals with tax avoidance in a number of ways, particularly pertaining to when an 'abuse' is identified. Some specific provisions can make a tax scheme illegal. This applies to schemes entered into with the sole or dominant purpose of obtaining a tax benefit.

When it was introduced, the Income Tax Assessment Act stated:

- Arrangements of a normal business or family kind, including those of a tax planning nature, would be beyond its scope

- It is designed to operate against 'blatant, artificial, or contrived arrangements, but not cast unnecessary inhibitions on normal commercial transactions by which taxpayers legitimately take advantage of opportunities available for the arrangement of their affairs'[28]

Kinds of tax

Our taxes can be distilled into two parts.

Income tax

Income tax is worked out by reference to the taxable income of a taxpayer for the financial year.

Taxable income = assessable income – deductions

Assessable income consists of income which is ordinary or statutory in nature:

---

28 J Stephenson, 'Tax avoidance after Spotless' (Parliament of Australia, 30 June 1997), www.aph.gov.au / About_Parliament / Parliamentary_ Departments / Parliamentary_Library / pubs / rp / RP9697 / 97rp21, accessed 14 January 2021

- Ordinary income – earnings from personal services (salary, wage, director fee), business income, interest received, rents and dividends

- Statutory income – amounts that are made assessable income by specific provisions in the law, such as making a net capital gain on an investment

  Tax payable = gross tax – tax offsets

The gross tax of an individual, business or entity is calculated according to the scale or tax rate (excluding Medicare). Examples of tax offsets are the low-income, the private health insurance, the franking credit and the foreign-income offset.

Income tax deductions

A general deduction is any loss or outgoing that is incurred in gaining or producing assessable income, or is necessarily incurred in carrying on a business for income producing purposes. A loss or outgoing may be deductible even though it does not produce assessable income in the year in which it is incurred.

A specific deduction is an expense which is deductible under specific provisions in the law, such as for repairs, prior year's losses (CGT), partnership loss or depreciation. Employees and self-employed persons are entitled to deductions for expenditure incurred in gaining or producing assessable income. Common examples are:

- Cost of renegotiating an employment contract

- Cost of travelling between two or more different places of work

- Depreciation on computers used for work

- Technical journals

- Membership of unions or professional associations

- Tax return preparation

- Donations

- Self-education expenses if your self-education relates to your current work activities as an employee

Capital gains tax

There are a number of 'events' that constitute a capital gain, most of which come down to the sale of an asset or a change in its beneficial ownership. A capital gain asset includes any form of property and any legal or equitable right.

There will be a capital gain if the proceeds from the sale of an investment exceed its cost base (the price you first paid for that investment, eg a share in a company or unit in a trust). Likewise, there will be a capital loss if what you receive from the trade of an investment is less than its original cost base. The net difference between a gain and loss forms part of your assessable income. You can also carry forward previous years' losses in your tax return. Your accountant is the best person to calculate your capital gain liability and how it forms a part of your assessable income.

It is important to know when a CGT event occurs, because:

- Events involving assets acquired before 20 September 1985 are generally exempt from CGT rules

- The timing of the event and date the asset was purchased may allow for indexation calculations

- The timing may affect the tax year in which the CGT gain / loss is taken into account

I strongly recommend that you visit your accountant or registered tax agent for more information. They will be able to collaborate with your advisor.

Ways to own assets

A breakdown of the tax rate for different entities is best illustrated in this table:

Table 6.1: Entity tax breakdown

	Income	Capital gains
Individual	Marginal rates (0–45% + Medicare)	Under twelve months = 0–46.5% Over twelve months 0–23.5%
Trust	Assessed at the rate of a beneficiary	Assessed at the rate of a beneficiary
Company	30% 27.5% (lower company tax rate)	30% (no discount)
Superannuation fund (Acc.)	15%	Under twelve months = 15% Over twelve months = 10%
Superannuation fund (account-based pension – ABP)	0%	0%

THE TAO OF WEALTH AND PROSPERITY

Individual

The simplest structure through which to own an asset is in the name of an individual. There are no restrictions on obtaining access to the income and capital or claiming a deduction on your earnings.

Advantages:

- It's simple.

- There is no additional administrative time or cost.

- The 50% CGT discount applies if the asset has been held for a minimum of twelve months.

- You can claim a full tax deduction for superannuation contributions up to the contribution limits.

Disadvantages:

- There is no asset protection.

- Income is taxed at rates of up to 49%.

Company

A company is a separate legal entity. It owns assets in its own right. It can enter into contracts, be sued and take legal action.

A company is generally used:

- As a vehicle to carry on a business

- As the trustee of a trust or self-managed super fund

- As the beneficiary of a discretionary family trust

One of the greatest advantages of a company is that it gives the shareholders limited liability. Their liability for the debts of the company is limited to the amount of capital they have subscribed to the company. The shareholders cannot be personally sued for the liabilities of the company.

The company is treated as a separate entity for tax purposes – it pays a flat tax rate of 30% (or 27.5% if turnover is less than $50 million). Note that companies are not eligible for the CGT discount and all capital gains are still taxed at a flat rate.

It is a unique feature of the Australian tax law that under the imputation system, the shareholders are entitled to a tax credit for the underlying income tax paid by the company – this is known as franking credits. The effect of the franking system is that the portion of the net income of the company distributed as dividends is taxed at the investor's marginal rate.

Advantages:

- A company has limited liability.

- Company income is taxed at the relatively low flat rate of 27.5% for small business entities or 30% for all other companies.

- A company can stream pre-tax income through the payment of reasonable salaries.

- Shareholders can receive fully franked dividends (Australian companies only).

- A company that carries on a business and has shareholders, if they have a significant interest, can make maximum use of the CGT small business concessions.

Disadvantages:

- A company has higher set-up costs than other structures.

- There are administrative requirements to advise ASIC of any changes to the company structure.

- A company structure can enable clients to defer tax, but ultimately, if a person wishes to access the money that is in the company, a dividend will need to be paid.

- A company cannot claim the 50% CGT discount.

- Losses incurred by a company are trapped within that company; only the company can carry those losses forward and they are not passed on to shareholders.

Consult with an accountant when considering the establishment of a company and the legal implications.

Trust

A trust is a separate entity in which a trustee holds property and income on behalf of its beneficiaries. Beneficiaries ultimately entitled to receive and retain trust income carry a personal tax liability when the income is distributed from the trust.

The unique feature of a trust structure is that the assets are controlled by one or more persons, and in some cases (family trust) there is discretion as to how resources are allotted to each beneficiary. This makes it a very effective tax planning vehicle when the need arises.

A trust would generally be used by individuals who wish to:

- Maintain control of their investments and have the ability to tax-effectively stream the income/capital gains between family members

- Run a family business

- Protect their assets

A trust is founded by a settlor and an appointer – each has their own respective responsibilities, which your solicitor and accountant will be able to explain. The main parties to a trust are:

- **The trustee**, who is the legal owner of the trust assets, responsible for payments to the beneficiaries and vesting the property in the beneficiaries on termination of the trust. It is common for a company to be the trustee.

- **Trust property.** A trust must have trust property, but this may be tangible or intangible. It includes assets, real estate, cash, equities, bonds or companies operated by a business owner (shareholder).

- **A beneficiary** can be a company, another trust or individuals. Beneficiaries can be entitled to income, capital or both. For discretionary trusts, the list of beneficiaries is usually wide. It will include children, grandchildren, family companies, other family trusts and charities.

Special forms of trust include child maintenance, special disability, testamentary and unit trusts. Your accountant and solicitor can go through these in detail if the circumstances arise. Refer to the estate planning chapter (Chapter 3) for the use of testamentary trusts.

Advantages:

- Complete flexibility in relation to income splitting (a trust can use tax rates of individuals and companies).

- The ability to stream different types of income to different beneficiaries.

- The ability to stream capital gains to different beneficiaries.

- The availability of the 50% CGT discount.

- The ability to make superannuation contributions up to concessional cap.

- Protection of assets.

- The ability to contribute to estate planning.

Disadvantages:

- It's complicated to understand.

- There are moderate set-up costs.

- There are administration costs (you need to lodge a separate tax return and maintain a separate bank account for a trust).

- Tax losses are quarantined within the trust.

Superannuation

Your superannuation account is a special form of trust governed by the Superannuation Industry (Supervision) (SIS) Act. There are covenants surrounding your super and it is used to save for your retirement as a substitute for the age pension. Refer to Part 2:

'Superannuation' for more information on how to optimise your retirement.

BRETT AND ANDREA'S STORY

Brett (fifty-five) was an operations manager of a packaging company; his wife Andrea (fifty-four) worked a couple of days at the local chemist and helped with running the household. They had two children, a son in Year 12 and the other finishing his first year of university.

Brett's main focus was kicking goals at work and spending time with his family. Andrea's concerns were centred on helping their children enter into the Sydney property market. Brett was incredibly driven, while Andrea was extremely caring. They were both sensitive and protective of their finances, and investing was an emotional decision for them, especially where they believed there would be a high degree of change. A small deviation in their routine evoked an emotional trigger because it involved a new operating framework.

Their objective was to help their children buy their first homes and retire at sixty. This was something that they were already likely to achieve with the amount of cash they were saving each year, and Brett was on a high income. They were able to pay down their house quickly and accrue a cash saving of $2,000,000 held in Andrea's name.

As Andrea had mostly focused on her home duties, she hadn't contributed much to her superannuation account and had only amounted a sum of $20,000 in her fund. Brett, on the other hand, had reached the transfer balance cap and had over $1.6 million in his superannuation. When we determined their asset allocation, they were incredibly risk averse.

Table 6.2: Balance sheet after advice

Investment	Owner	Assets	Liabilities
Home	Joint	$1,000,000	0
Cash	Andrea	$2,000,000	
Super	Brett	$1,650,000	
Super	Andrea	$20,000	
		$4,670,000	

The strategy was to establish a family trust which invested the $2,000,000 of cash held in Andrea's name. Any income from the trust could be distributed between the adult children and Andrea.

I recommended that Andrea establish a second superannuation fund for non-concessional contributions ($100,000 each year) while maximising her concessional contribution cap in her existing super fund, thus quarantining the components. This same contribution strategy for Andrea could be repeated until she turned sixty-five or reached the transfer balance cap. At the same time, because Andrea could access her superannuation in six years' time, the concessional contributions she made to her existing super fund could be invested in a lower tax structure, and then withdrawn at a later date (tax free) to purchase a home for both children.

Table 6.3: Balance sheet after Year 1 of advice[29]

Investment	Owner	Assets	Liabilities
Home	Joint	$1,000,000	0
Conservative investments	Family trust	$2,000,000	
Super	Brett	$1,650,000	
Super 1	Andrea	$100,000	
Super 2	Andrea	$45,000	
		$4,795,000	

Table 6.4: Income, tax and distributions from family trust[30]

	Brett	Andrea	Child 1	Total
Income	$400,000	$75,000	$25,000	$500,000
Personal deductible contribution	$0	$25,000	$0	$25,000
Taxable income	$400,000	$75,000	$25,000	$475,000
Tax on income	($153,097)	($7,797)	($1,292)	($167,036)
Medicare levy	($8,000)	($1,000)	($500)	($9,500)

Continued

---

29 Assuming that the conservative investments earned 5%.
30 The table shows the amount of tax and Medicare levy payable between a personal salary and distributions from a family trust. More importantly, it's how much cash is available after tax to fund a cost of living. A financial advisor will have access to software that will automatically calculate your tax position tax rates from the financial year 2019–20.

Table 6.4 cont.

	Brett	Andrea	Child 1	Total
Total tax payable	($161,097)	($8,797)	($1,792)	($171,686)
Total cash flow	$238,903	$66,203	$23,208	$328,314

The error that they made was that they should have started sooner! They weren't contributing to Andrea's super account and didn't invest; they just held funds in cash for ten years as they were risk averse and had missed out on the opportunity of investing $2 million over that period of time. Had they started earlier, they could have invested in a lower tax structure and probably doubled their wealth. They would have had sufficient capital to adequately retire at fifty-five. Instead, they chose to avoid making decisions and stuck to the status quo.

Brett and Andrea, unaccustomed to change, could just as easily have achieved the goal of placing a deposit on houses for their children had they stuck to their guns. Their main concern was performance in both up and down markets (but mostly down markets), and they also worried about losing what they had previously gained. But they ended up caught in an analysis paralysis; doing nothing cost them a huge opportunity.

The Tao of tax

Tax is a topic that is highly charged. In Australia, we have a 'progressive' tax system, where the more you earn, the more you are required to pay. And the more you spend, the more you pay in goods and service tax (GST).

The common objective of tax is to help others and effectively allocate resources that prevent crime and stop disease. But our politicians and media commentators love to shout at one another about this very issue; it is the catalyst for much noise and many scare campaigns which don't provide an inkling of service or time spent helping.

It can't be denied that higher taxation does have negative consequences. It has the capacity to distort prices and markets, and arguably waives individual incentives, but as Australians, we have the ability to use our taxes in the form of a GST (what you spend is what you pay) and there is an alignment between federal, state and local governments. We can take pride in what we have built, how we take care of the elderly and the less fortunate, and how we create a better future that is in line with our civic values of mateship and equal opportunity.

A society, like the pub, is there to be shared and its welfare is for the benefit of all. Too much or too little tax is just like having too much to drink or being the boring sober guy at a party; it's better to strike a happy medium where everyone can get along just fine, sing and dance the night away while still getting home safely.

Summary

While most people agree that tax creates a better society for all of us, they would also agree that minimising the tax they pay where they can is worthwhile.

When you're structuring your finances, it's important to understand the tax obligations and implications for each choice you make. You need to be clear on whether you're required to pay tax and the kinds of tax you're required to pay. Know all your options for asset ownership, whether they be individual, company, trust or superannuation, as well as the tax advantages and disadvantages of each.

When it comes to minimising your tax each year, keep in mind Australia's greatest ever band – AC/DC:

- Anti-avoidance
- Calculate your income
- Deduct your expenses
- Check with your accountant and advisor

7
Managing Debt And
The Cost Of A Household

For many people looking to start a family and go about their daily lives, mortgage and debt can prove to be a huge burden. But even when you feel trapped in debt, there are options open to you.

In this chapter, we'll look at the functions of debt and how to use it wisely. We'll discover how entrepreneurs use debt to power our society and the difference between healthy and unhealthy debt. Next, we'll explore ways to recycle debt, such as your mortgage, to leverage it for different financial strategies. Finally, we'll discuss the importance of thinking about debt creatively – the Tao of debt.

Using debt wisely

Debt is a necessary function of an economy that can have a polarising effect on your financial position. Good debt, structured wisely, can accelerate your wealth creation, while bad debt is detrimental to your financial wellbeing.

If you make prudent financial decisions in the medium and long term, and maintain a long-term investment horizon, you can leverage debt to accelerate your wealth and capital, while at the same time minimising your income tax. These strategies may be suited to a young family sorting things out, or an established business owner who is aiming to create more time, grow capital for an early retirement, pay off the mortgage or provide children with the best possible education.

Debt and the entrepreneur

Before we look into the different kinds of debt and how you might manage your relationship with it, let's take a quick detour to examine how entrepreneurs use debt, and how vital their use of debt is to our economy and society.

The role of entrepreneurs is akin to the eyes of the society. They are forward looking and believe that the future will be better. Our entire banking system is designed to issue credit and living standards depend on access to this credit, so loans can be made available for entrepreneurs who wish to start a business.

As Adam Smith explained in his book *The Wealth of Nations*,[31] first published in 1776, the role of the entrepreneur is to establish a new solution or product that benefits themselves and the lives of others. Society benefits from innovation, as the entrepreneur takes on all the risk, in exchange offering their intellectual property for money and increasing the standard of living for the common good, which explains why value creation is asymmetrical. A few people inherit the risk, produce the most results and are rewarded. Results and value go hand in hand.

Increases in the profits of private entrepreneurs are the fundamental engine of the capitalist system. Everybody's prosperity and collective wealth is determined by productivity (labour and capital). For every dollar that is loaned out, the entrepreneur must pay interest on the loan, and in return for depositing money in the bank to loan to the entrepreneur, savers earn interest.

It is through the sacrifice of intellectual property and labour that the entrepreneur has the ability to generate capital. Success means that the entrepreneur will be able to pay their employees a wage or invest in new technologies. Failure implies that they are unable to

---

31 A Smith, *The Wealth of Nations: The economics classic* (Bibliomania.
    com, Oxford, England, 2002), retrieved from the Library of Congress,
    www.loc.gov/item/2002564559, accessed 14 January 2021

repay their loans and become bankrupt. The bank will then charge more interest on its loans and provide less in return for savers, and the difference between these rates is essentially how banks are profitable.

Living standards increase due to the manifestation of a competitive marketplace. Businesses generate employment and savings that are deposited in banks, which in turn issue secondary loans for people looking to purchase a home. Without an entrepreneur's vision, innovation will not happen and society will not benefit from their skillset, intellectual property and an increase in living standards.

Debt in the hands of those willing to assume its risks is a vital engine of our society. Without it, our economies would stagnate. But it's important to understand the difference between healthy generative debt and unhealthy debilitating debt.

Debt and the theory of relativity

Like the Newtonian laws of a budget that we discussed in Chapter 2, we can think of debt as a matter of physics – this time akin to Einstein's theory of relativity. The equivalence of mass and energy is summed up by $E = mc^2$, where E is energy, m is mass and c is the speed of light.

The essence of Einstein's theory of relativity is that the higher their mass and the pull of gravity, the harder it is for moving objects to move at speeds close to the speed of light, so time slows down. This is comparable to using debt to your advantage or disadvantage. Debt can be a burden which eventually must be repaid, or it can shape the way you use your time and grow a portfolio.

Consider this order of debts from heaviest to lightest. Which ones can augment your sense of time and dilate your goals?

Black hole

Unnecessary credit-card debt which you just can't seem to climb out of, instead using it to fund your cost of living, is the terrible black hole of debt. If you are struggling with personal debt and managing a budget, the best way to prioritise is to start by paying off the debt carrying the highest interest rate, then the next highest until you get rid of everything.

Red dwarf

Debts like car loans or equipment finance loans are OK in the short term, but look to pay these off in at least five years. Almost all businesses need a car or machinery/computers in a factory or an office. In most cases, the interest on this debt can be claimed as a deduction in some shape or form.

Eventually these assets, while they have an economic benefit, depreciate in value and have a limited shelf life. It's worth creating a strategy around them to pay them off within your means.

Neutron star

Your mortgage is a necessary debt – we all need a place to live and call home. The benefits of owning your home are that savings from any extra repayments can be compounded and the appreciation of the property will exceed the loan value. The opportunity cost of a mortgage is that repayments are traded off against a lost opportunity to invest in assets that would provide an additional income and increase your capital.

The Australian dream is to purchase a home on a quarter-acre block and pass it on from one generation to the next. This is the proviso for paying down the mortgage as quickly as possible.

Let me guess: you likely love your home. It's usually a joy to sit back and take on the quirks of family life from your little castle. But the mortgage repayments tend to occupy a significant portion of the family budget and it'll be a number of years before you can wave goodbye to the bank.

It's this trade-off that can preclude your eventual retirement objective and, in the short term, result in you paying too much tax. With the right approach, you can extinguish your mortgage a lot sooner than you may think and accelerate your wealth creation at the same time.

Supernova

Useful debt is that which can be leveraged or 'geared' to buy assets, invest and generate income/activity, accelerating achievement of your goals, though it does come with risk. Interest is tax deductible in full if the purpose of the loan is to produce future income.

It's important to note that adding leverage to any investment increases a loan's risk and the timeframe for investing. The success of this strategy depends on whether you expect the return from the investment, including both the income and capital gains after tax and expenses, to increase after the borrowing.

Debt recycling

A debt recycling strategy involves utilising the equity in your home for the purpose of investing. In doing so, you're able to pay off your mortgage sooner than its set term, and the interest you pay on your home loan is recycled from being non-deductible to a tax deduction. This strategy is typically associated with paying the same mortgage repayments each month while establishing a separate line of credit secured against the equity in your family home to invest into securities that are going to provide capital growth and additional income.

A debt recycling strategy and effective leveraging can be prudent ways to shave years off the mortgage (in many cases you can be mortgage free in just ten years), reduce your tax and grow your wealth. Using leverage as a means of borrowing to invest is commonly associated with the purchase of an investment property. It is also applicable to other assets which provide capital growth and income, such as domestic and international equities. By borrowing more to invest in a portfolio through a secured loan, you get amplified returns and additional income, and interest payable on a loan for investment purposes can be claimed as a tax deduction. By the end of a debt recycling strategy, you're still left with debt that has to be repaid, but the interest repayments have been transferred from non-deductible debt on your home to debt that is now deductible.

Portfolio or property?

The advantage of investing in a portfolio of assets, rather than just an investment property, is the liquidity of the portfolio. If you use your equity to buy an investment property, it's a lot of debt to take on at once. When you invest in a portfolio of domestic and international equities, you're able to take advantage of any securities that are undervalued, and dial up or dial down the investments depending on how you feel.

After a period of ten years, the end result is that you do have debt to your name, but you have a much larger asset base and additional income to begin paying off the loan. Your asset base and any extra income can also be restructured and redirected into your superannuation account through various contribution strategies. Not only do you pay off your mortgage faster than you may have hoped, you get to retire sooner.

If you have your heart set on buying an investment property, you're still able to do so, but it's better to have a portfolio that is properly diversified first. Then if your situation changes, you're able to mitigate any risks by selling down part of your portfolio rather than triggering a huge capital gains event.

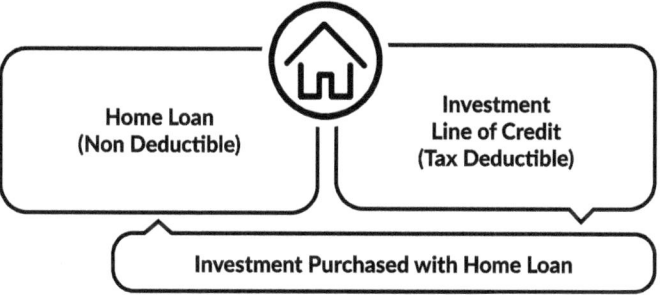

Gearing

A debt recycling strategy can be used as a means of positive, neutral or negative gearing. An investment property or portfolio is positively geared when the income it generates exceeds the interest repayments.

The positive income is then applied to your personal income.

A neutrally geared strategy implies that the interest repayments and income balance out. A negatively geared strategy implies that the interest repayments on the loan exceed the taxable income, so can be claimed as a tax deduction. If a debt recycling strategy is to be successful, the investor relies purely on the capital growth of the investment, and in the short term will have to suffer cash flow that is negative. As a result, the asset is subject to CGT when it is sold.

The concept of negative gearing has been bashed in the media and is subject to a lot of conjecture, particularly its impact on property prices. A negative gearing strategy is about picking your poison: you're either paying the bank more than you should be in interest, or paying income tax on the investment and hoping that the CGT you will be subject to at a point in the future is minimal.

Benefits and risks of recycling and gearing

A debt recycling strategy has its benefits, but there are increased risks as it requires a long timeframe to invest. This strategy is more beneficial to people in high-income brackets. Excessive gearing can prove financially disastrous, especially when an investor chases returns without understanding the whole financial picture.

Throughout nature, the organism on the path of least resistance is the most successful, just as in business, the lowest-cost producer is the most dominant in any industry. Table 7.1 summarises the benefits and risks – the path of least resistance – between investing in property and equities.

Leverage for education

Using leverage to magnify your income and grow your capital doesn't need to be considered in isolation. Quite often, you can use strategies pertaining to leverage to achieve the objective of funding a child's education.

According to the Australian Scholarships Group (ASG), in the past ten years there has been a sharp increase in the cost of education which has exceeded wages growth. Research completed by the ASG states, 'the estimated cost of a private education across metropolitan Australia has skyrocketed 61% or $180,128 in the past 10 years.'[32] With school fees occupying more of the family budget, money must be cut from other experiences.

---

32 'National: The cost of education growing faster than average wages' [media release] (ASG, 2018), www.asg.com.au/doc/default-source/2018-asg-planning-for-education-media-releases---australia/asg_2018-planning-for-education_national_approved.pdf?sfvrsn=2, accessed 4 January 2021

Table 7.1: Benefits and risks of properties and equities

	Property	Equities
Time to service	High	Low
Administration cost to serve	High	Low
	5% of rental income	Brokerage
	+ Strata fees	+ Management expense ratios (managed and exchange-traded funds)
	+ Insurance	
Tax effective	Low	High
	Deductions on depreciation	Franking credits (Aus. equities) – tax effective
	Land tax	International equities – withholding tax – insignificant
	Stamp duties	
Emotional attachment (anchoring)	High	Medium
Liquidity	Low	Very high
Time horizon to invest (strategy)	Long-term	Long-term
	(Buy and hold)	(Buy and hold)
Perceived risk	Low	High
Resistance level	High	Low

These tables show an overview of what parents can expect in relation to their child's education.

Table 7.2: Metropolitan areas around Australia – estimated schooling costs for child starting in 2019

Year		Government	Catholic	Independent
Prep	2019	$3,946	$5,581	$12,825
Year 1	2020	$4,047	$5,733	$13,203
Year 2	2021	$4,150	$5,890	$13,593
Year 3	2022	$4,256	$6,052	$13,995
Year 4	2023	$4,364	$6,218	$14,408
Year 5	2024	$4,476	$6,388	$14,834
Year 6	2025	$4,590	$6,563	$15,272
Year 7	2026	$6,063	$12,989	$30,626
Year 8	2027	$6,225	$13,414	$31,694
Year 9	2028	$6,392	$13,853	$32,801
Year 10	2029	$6,563	$14,307	$33,946
Year 11	2030	$6,738	$14,777	$35,132
Year 12	2031	$6,919	$15,262	$36,360
Total		**$68,729**	**$127,027**	**$298,689**

Table 7.3: Estimated schooling costs in Australian metropolitan areas

	Government		Catholic		Independent	
	Primary	Secondary	Primary	Secondary	Primary	Secondary
Tuition	$325	$673	$2,211	$6,477	$9,664	$19,556
Uniform	$292	$353	$436	$480	$327	$475
Devices	$782	$1,340	$956	$1,136	$323	$1,172
Excursions	$338	$436	$213	$334	$221	$508
Camps	$298	$472	$234	$338	$197	$500
Transport	$292	$344	$308	$515	$688	$562
Sports Apparel	$305	$322	$292	$320	$282	$369
Music Instruments	$377	$261	$295	$231	$453	$306
Extra Tuition	$936	$844	$636	$547	$670	$657
Total	**$3,945**	**$5,045**	**$5,581**	**$10,378**	**$12,825**	**$24,105**

The Tao of debt

The trick with debt is to think creatively. For advice, let's turn to Price's law, which explores the realms of creativity. Price's law is a variety of the Pareto principle,[33] where 20% of your output produces 80% of the results. In Price's analysis, the square root of the number of people in a domain produces 50% of its creative output.

According to Price's law:[34]

- In a company of ten people, three people do 50% of the creative work – 30% of the population

- In a company of 100 people, ten people perform 50% of the creative work – 10% of the population

- In a population of 1,000,000 people, 1,000 people perform 50% of the creative output = 0.1%

Price's law applies to every single realm where there is creative production. You don't become rich for thinking up ideas; you become rich by making them into a reality – small steps lead to leaps. It's the few people who create the most and are paid for that responsibility.

---

33 JB Peterson, *12 Rules For Life: An antidote to chaos* (Penguin Random House, New York, 2018), pp8–9
34 JB Peterson, '2017 Personality 19: biology & traits: openness/ intelligence/creativity II' (2 May 2017), www.youtube.com/ watch?v=fjtBDa4aSGM

This reoccurs throughout nature, from the size of trees in a forest to the mass of stars. In a hive, the queen bee gets all the honey and everyone else does the repetitive or unitary tasks. What Price's law suggests is that life is a series of trading games in every single domain. It then becomes a question of how we find our own lane and achieve optimal results.

Sometimes, we need to think creatively, even if we're in the minority, to be the most productive. It is a matter of putting ourselves in a position for our own interests, of focusing on the important things, so that we can be as productive and creative as possible in line with our values, merit and engagement. And, of course, we must be willing to accept the consequences.

Summary

Not all debt is bad. As we have seen in this chapter, there are many kinds of debt, from the black hole of the credit card to the supernova of recycling. It's important to understand the differences and know when debt is working for us and when it is working against us.

Debt can be used to your advantage if it is managed within your means. Adding leverage to an investment portfolio, whether it is property or shares, will amplify your returns and capital appreciation and magnify your income. The objective of using leverage is primarily to make more money and accelerate your wealth creation, so it's important to consider the long-term CGT consequences, benefits and risks to each asset class.

For further consideration, consult a mortgage broker and accountant about the types of loans available to you, and various ways that debt can be structured effectively between entities such as a company, family trust and SMSFs. For more information about investing for a child's education and using leverage to pay off your mortgage, visit the resource section and download a copy of the brochure *Pay off the Mortgage and Send Your Kids to the Best School* at www. equanimityfs.com.au / resources.

PART FOUR
ASSETS, CAPITAL AND THE MARKET

8
Focus On Capital

Rarely is there anything 'new' in finance and economics. Your asset allocation is the fundamental determinant of how much money you can make over a period of time, it's that simple. But nothing in life is without a risk or trade-off.

In this chapter, I am going to introduce the basics of diversification and the considerations, benefits and risks of each major asset class. We'll look at the way assets are classed according to their risks and rewards, examining defensive assets such as cash bonds and hybrids, growth assets such as Australian equities, property and international equities, as well as alternative assets such as hedge funds, venture capital and options and derivatives. We'll go through the pros and cons of each, and finally take a look at the way our human emotions can become fatally entangled in all our best-laid business plans.

Your advisor's role is not to be a professional fund manager or stock picker; he or she outsources that to fund managers. Rather, your advisor will select the most important types of investment vehicles that are applicable to your goals and objectives. Their role is to ensure that you have the right asset allocation and suitable structures that will enable you to achieve your financial and lifestyle goals.

Risk vs reward

When we consider investing, we focus on building capital. Remember, we're always going to be better off being equity rich and cash-flow poor, rather than earning lots and spending it all straight away.

Money is a medium of exchange or a store of value. It can be likened to fruit (income) from a tree (capital). There will always be economic times of summer, winter, spring and autumn, so it's important that we build our orchard to cope with all the seasons. When it comes to money, the more risk we take, the higher the reward we stand to make, but every investment has its risk. The best way to mitigate these risks is to diversify. As the old proverb warns – don't put all of your eggs in one basket.

The major asset classes available to you and their relative risks and rewards are shown in the graph below.

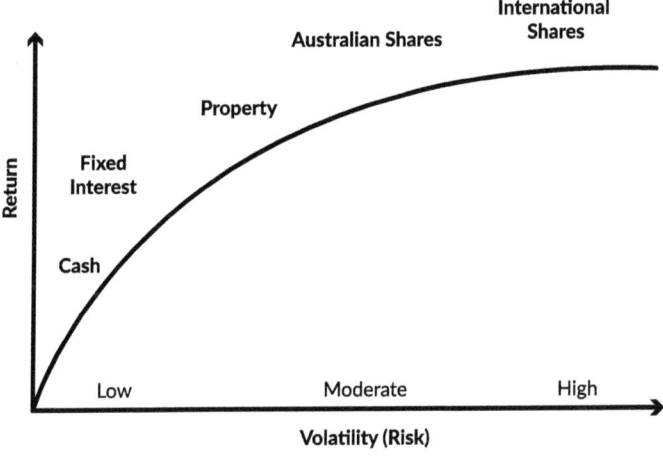

For the purpose of simplicity, the risk vs reward trade-off can be lumped into three categories:

- Defensive
- Growth
- Alternatives

Defensive assets

These types of assets are designed to pay a regular income in the form of interest. They are characterised by investing in short-term horizons (up to five years) and their value generally does not fluctuate greatly.

Cash and term deposits

This is money in bank accounts and the notes resting in your wallet. It is what it is – best used to exchange for goods and services or to have on hand in case of an emergency. You will be paid interest for holding funds in an account.

Benefits:

- Liquidity and accessibility.

- Available in case of emergency or to buy more shares or bonds in the event of a downturn.

Risks:

- Inflation will rob you of your purchasing power as these deposits pay a low interest rate – over long periods of time, your cash will be worth less.

Bonds

A bond is a debt instrument or a loan from the issuer to a party (an IOU).[35] Consider it a fixed income investment where one party promises to pay a series of interest payments in fixed amounts and the principal at maturity.

---

35 A Robbins, *Money – Master The Game: 7 simple steps to financial freedom* (Simon & Schuster, New York, 2014)

Bonds are rated on the probability of default (failure to make promised payments). Lower yielding bonds have a lower probability of default while higher yielding bonds carry a greater risk.

Examples of bonds include:

- Floating rate notes

- Corporate bonds

- Government bonds (Australian government bonds or US treasury bonds)

- Non-sovereign/state bonds (Queensland or NSW governments)

- Mortgage-backed securities

In instances where a company or government becomes insolvent, bond holders are the first order of creditors to be repaid.

Benefits:

- Pays a guaranteed income.

- Corporate bond holders get paid out first in the case of bankruptcy.

- Liquidity – most bonds are commonly and readily tradable.

Risks:

- Duration – interest rates may affect the value of the bond.

- Agency risk (depends on the issuer's ability to repay the loan and credit rating).

- Currency denomination may have unforeseen implications on a portfolio.

Bonds can be confusing – just because the income is guaranteed doesn't necessarily mean it is without risk. Like an antique weight scale, bonds increase in value when interest rates go down, and decrease in value when interest rates go up.

Hybrids and convertible notes

Hybrids combine elements of debt and equity securities. Hybrid securities typically promise to pay a rate of return (fixed or floating) until a certain date, in the same way debt securities do, but they also have equity-like features that mean they may provide a higher rate of return than regular debt securities. This is due to the higher inherent risk of these equity-like features – if a company were to become insolvent, the people holding preference shares/hybrids are paid after bond holders have been paid.

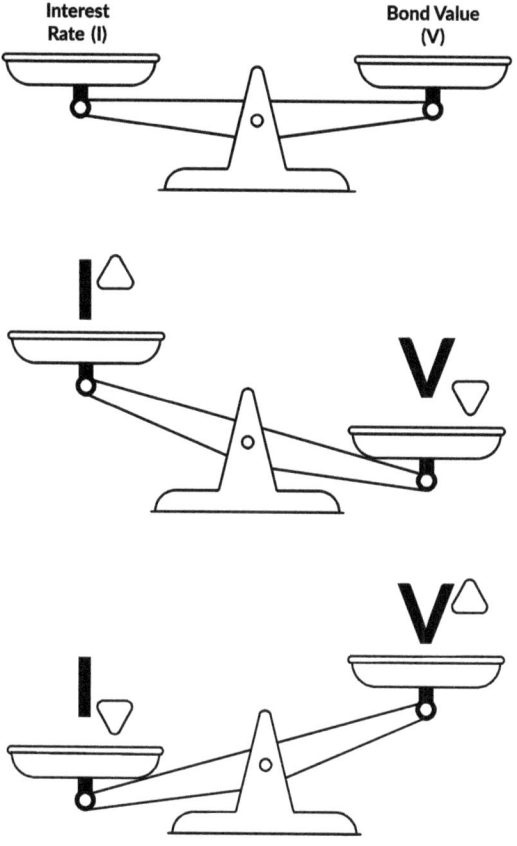

Benefits:

- Hybrids pay a guaranteed dividend which may be greater than that of ordinary shareholders.

- They may be entitled to franking credits.

- Liquidity – they're traded on the stock exchange.

Risks:

- Hybrids may be converted to equity or terminated at a time not beneficial to the holder.

Growth assets

Growth-oriented asset classes are those that increase in capital value over time. They can exhibit more volatility in the short term, but in the long run, they provide a higher rate of return. Ultimately, volatility is the price you pay for capital growth.

Australian equities

An Australian share is a part ownership of a public company listed on the Australian Stock Exchange (ASX). Equities pay dividends, and in Australia, part of the existing tax that has been paid from the company can be rebated to an individual (or entity) in the form of a franking credit.

Common shareholders have a residual claim (after debt holders and preferred stockholders) on a firm's assets if the firm is liquidated. Shareholders also govern the corporation through voting rights. Typically, shareholders vote on boards of directors, merger decisions and the selection of auditors. If unable to do so in person, shareholders can cast their vote by proxy.

Australian shares are popular for their tendency to pay a high yield or dividend. The market has traditionally been dominated by mining and banking, and the top twenty stocks of the ASX account for approximately 70% of the index's market cap. These shares consistently pay out between 70% and 80% of profits as dividends.

Exposure to the Australian stock market will have its benefits due to the consistency of returns and tax perks. This enables investors' portfolios to maintain purchasing power relative to other assets and the cost of living.

Benefits:

- Long-term capital growth.

- Renowned for paying dividends.

- Franking credits and tax effectiveness.

- Liquidity – trade plus two days.

- Cheap to administer.

Risks:

- Limited in exposure and risk being capped due to market share.

- The ASX makes up 2% of total equity markets in the world.

- The ASX is traditionally concentrated on blue-chip stocks which are limited to the sectors of banking and mining.

- Like all equities, stocks are volatile in the short term.

Property

Property ownership can be achieved either directly or indirectly. Direct property ownership gives the investor full control and responsibility for the management of the actual property. Indirect property ownership typically involves making an investment through a fund that in turn invests in one or more underlying properties that can be listed on the ASX or through a managed fund.

Common property examples include:

- Australian real estate trusts (listed on ASX)

- Global real estate trusts (listed on global exchanges)

- Direct property (residential or commercial)

As a rule of thumb, the benefits and risks of investing in direct property are summarised below.

Benefits:

- Hedge against inflation.

- Provides long-term capital growth.

- Pays income in the form of rent.

- You can claim tax deductions such as strata, depreciation and repairs.

- Your primary residence is exempt from any capital gains.

- Using leverage as a means to renovate a property can magnify returns/rental income.

Risks:

- Liquidity – you can't sell half of your investment property. The success of your investment is limited to your timing and the capital growth of the investment. You won't know whether the profit was worth your time until after you buy, sell and calculate the costs and tax.

- Not always tax effective (land tax and council rates).

- Costly to administer. Usually a landlord will take 5% of rental income, which is expensive compared to other investment costs. You may be subject to strata and insurance.

- Confined to local demographics and economies of an area, and demand for certain property type (apartment vs house).

- Bad tenants.

- Maintenance.

- There are only expensive lessons.

Financial advisors aren't property specialists – they can only provide advice around property securities listed on the ASX or via a managed fund. Like all asset classes or investments, a return is never guaranteed: there are only benefits and risks.

Investing in property does have its unforeseen risks: when you renovate a property or apartment and things go wrong, they go badly wrong. There are no small mistakes, only expensive lessons (just ask a gyprocker or roof tiler).

Throughout my career, people have asked me for advice on buying an investment property. Of all Australians, 70% do not invest in property, and 1% of people own three properties or more.[36] Property carries a high degree of emotional attachment as it's associated with safety, protection and the happiness of a family home. People naturally desire to own their own home instead of having to rent.

If that is the path you would like to take and you have your heart set in stone about renovating and owning an investment property, by all means go for it and I wish you the best of luck. The builder's bug can be just as exciting as the stock market! But don't let an

---

36   B Martin, *The Freedom Formula: Live more, work less and leave a legacy with property* (Michael Hanrahan Publishing, Victoria, 2018)

emotional attachment to property and borrowing to renovate distort your judgement. By using leverage to invest, you're essentially increasing the risk, although the more you risk and the more you borrow, the more you stand to gain.

Regardless of the merits of investing in property, it is still subject to gross generalisations and sweeping statements. No asset class is immune from human-kind's tendency towards greed and wishful thinking. The crucial issue is not about chasing returns but tim-ing the market. Your return on direct property owner-ship is a function of how effectively you can renovate and 'flip' a dwelling. Given that you are leveraging into an investment, any gain or loss will make a mate-rial difference to your net wealth. You must examine real benefit versus the risks. In the short term, prop-erty and shares appreciate differently, but over time, they can even out, depending on how you view the data. Every asset class operates on a cycle; the main distinction with the property cycle is that there is a long lead time for development to take place (zoning, approvals, development), which can cause significant delays, thus putting downward pressure on prices if demand for dwellings is not met. And market condi-tions can change significantly in the interim.

Relying on macro-economic growth and demograph-ics to drive up an asset's value is anyone's guessing game; it is not comparable to analysing the intrinsic value of a share. But you do have to assess some things when evaluating a property:

- The property type (apartment, townhouse, house or studio)

- Location, location, location

- Success ultimately depends on your ability to pay off the loan as quickly as possible

- Local demographics and economies (eg the incomes of people living in NSW's south coast vs Sydney vs New York)

The property market is framed in sensational terms in the media with headlines like 'Home prices are unaffordable' or 'The only way to get rich is investing in property'. This can affect us on an emotional level. Everyone needs a place to live and the ownership rules governing our primary residence are attractive. Our family home is deemed tax free and is not subject to capital gains.

In his book *Irrational Exuberance*, Nobel Prize-winning economist Robert Shiller found, after adjusting for inflation, that US home prices have been nearly flat for the best part of a century.[37] The essence of Shiller's finding is that the best time to make money on property is during a bubble, but what happens after a bubble?

---

37 RJ Shiller, *Irrational Exuberance*, 3rd edition (Princeton University Press, New Jersey, 2016)

This finding is also relevant to the Australian property market. Nigel Stapledon from the University of New South Wales, who did his PhD on Melbourne property prices, found that the average return on property after inflation was 2.1%.[38] This doesn't include land taxes, interest repayments to the bank or renovations done to the home.[39]

I am not here to argue against the merits of investing in direct property, but rather to put it into perspective.

Property operates on a cycle just like equities or any other business. If you held the same amount of leverage in an Australian share portfolio as you hold in property for the same period, you would likely achieve the same result, if not something better. With an investment property, you also have to add in all the running costs (maintenance, council rates, strata, agent fees, CGT, income tax, loan/interest repayments) before calculating your profit, the net result of which will determine how successful the investment was. When investing in a property, you are leveraging in a single suburb of a single city in a single sub-asset class of an asset class, relying on a tenant and competing among the likes of Google and Amazon. Be careful!

---

38 N Stapledon, 'The inexorable rise in house prices in Australia since 1970: Unique or not?', *Australian Economic Review*, 49: 3 (2016), pp317–327

39 S Pape, *The Barefoot Investor: The only money guide you'll ever need* (Wiley, Milton, 2017)

In an economic downturn such as the GFC or the coronavirus pandemic, it is quite often property funds that are the hardest hit. As these funds are unit-trust structures, investors can get seriously burned by not being able to liquidate their investment, and in some cases, funds have frozen as it is impossible to sell a building or commercial property quickly.

There certainly is a position for investing in direct property in a portfolio. Ultimately, it's down to you and your understanding of the order of operations when it comes to achieving your long-term financial goals. It's my judgement that the success of a property can only be taken into consideration for a particular investment, not the asset class as a whole. Price is what you pay, value is what you get.

Also, you must put the long-term investment journey into perspective. It's difficult to 'in specie' a property into your superannuation fund (ie add it in as an asset, rather than as cash), so it's worth considering putting together a portfolio of listed securities first to grow and compound over time. That way, you are in a position to benefit from the liquid nature of those asset classes to mitigate the cost base when it comes to reducing a capital gain event. Once you have successfully put together a portfolio of securities, then it is worthwhile considering an investment property to magnify your income and provide a long-term hedge against inflation.

International equities

Developed markets

International equities in developed markets include shares in companies listed on exchanges such as those in New York (NSE), London (FTSE), Japan (Nikkei), Germany (DAX) and Paris (CAC). Companies listed on these exchanges obey the rules of their exchange and the sovereignty of their respective governments, so the risk of investing in overseas shares is not just confined to volatility. Fluctuations in currencies can also alter your portfolio performance.

Benefits:

- Exposure to companies that have earnings and operate all over the world.

- Certain sectors (eg tech/artificial intelligence) have a competitive advantage and are more innovative compared to companies trading in Australia.

- Difference in tax rates may make some companies more competitive and profitable.

- Movements in currency can be advantageous to a home-domiciled country.

- Long-term capital growth.

Risks:

- Volatility.

- The company may not pay a dividend, focusing on absolute return/capital appreciation of the security (eg Amazon).

- Fluctuations in currency can alter a portfolio's valuation.

Emerging markets

Emerging markets carry a higher degree of risk for a variety of reasons. In these markets, we are now seeing an emergence of a middle class as demographics are changing and people are introduced to more credit. While investing in emerging economies is volatile and subject to extreme fluctuations in currencies, they are durable and have an uncanny ability to absorb these pressures.

Benefits:

- Emerging and pre-emerging economies account for over 80% of the world's population (ie consumers and labour resources) and over 75% of the world's landmass (ie natural resources). In current exchange-rate terms, these countries account for around 40–50% of total world economic output.

- Over a long time period, these countries' economies have consistently grown faster than their developed counterparts and there is an expanding middle class.

Risks:

- Equities in emerging markets are a lot more volatile than traditional equities.

- The economies are subject to extreme fluctuations in currency.

- Legacy issues and, in some cases, opaque reporting standards and ineffectual governance arise.

Alternative assets

Alternative asset classes belong in a category of their own as they are neither a growth nor defensive asset. This type of asset class may include:

- Hedge funds (or 'funds of funds')

- Private equity

- Venture capital

- Options and derivatives

- Futures/forward contracts

- Commodities

These types of investments don't pay an income and are usually a bet/speculation on a certain event. You will only realise the value when that event occurs. For these investments, the perception of performance is subjective, varying according to the eyes of the investor.

Benefits:

• They can be useful instruments to hedge against inflation and insure against movements in a specified currency or commodity.

Risks:

• Quite often expensive in a portfolio.

• A hedge 'fund of funds' usually has a high internal rate of return, and on a risk-adjusted return basis, it's more often than not better to keep it simple.

The Tao of capital

What is it about money that is important to you? Money is an enabler and can serve, connect or divert you from your intentions. The decisions we all made about money five years ago brought us to the financial situation we are experiencing in the present moment.

The last step of the 5Cs, 'Continue', applies to the idea that it's possible to weather any financial storm or economic winter. But to do this, sometimes we must look beyond the noise. Humans tend to operate as a herd and like to follow a leader. As a result, bubbles and false prophets can lead us to unintended consequences in the short term, while in the long term we adapt and adjust.

Markets are fundamentally driven by emotion. As we're all human, we're all prone to overconfidence and error. Nobody has a crystal ball to say when the next boom or bust is going to be.

The term 'black swan' means an unexpected event which impacts financial systems (because naturalists once believed that all swans were white). Then Dutch explorers discovered an abundance of black swans in Australia. Nicholas Taleb in his book *The Black Swan* stated that in a perfect world, according to his mathematics, a financial crisis should occur every forty-four years.[40] But the reality is that humans are 'predictably irrational' and a bubble of a particular asset class occurs much more frequently, on average every three to four years.

Let's look at the ways that human emotions have historically led to market disasters.

---

40 NN Taleb, *The Black Swan: the impact of the highly improbable* (Random House, New York, 2007)

The Minsky Cycle

American economist Hyman Minsky described the formation of a bubble and the following crisis in five stages:[41]

1. Displacement – the birth of a boom, where some businesses fail and cease production, while others are immune to the shock and will exploit new opportunities or entrepreneurs will innovate new products as confidence slowly grows.

2. Credit creation – just as plants require sunlight to photosynthesise, we humans need access to credit to maintain or increase our living standards and for companies to bloom. As economies expand, we see an increase in employment, consumer spending and business investment. As the expansion reaches its peak, the rates of increase in spending, investment and employment slow, but inflation accelerates.

3. Euphoria – everyone starts to buy into the new era; everything is 'going up'. A wave of over-optimism and overconfidence is unleashed and the risks are underestimated.

4. Critical stage / financial distress. This is the Minsky moment. The bubble bursts, insiders quickly cash out, and this is followed by a financial crash. The Minsky moment occurs when credit and too much

---

41   J Montier, *The Little Book of Behavioural Investing: How not to be your own worst enemy* (John Wiley & Sons, New Jersey, 2010)

leverage have become a major problem. Fraud is another common denominator in this situation (the best example being the GFC).

5. Revulsion – investors are so scarred by recent events (in which they participated) that they can no longer bear to be in the market at all. There's bloodshed on markets, people get laid off from jobs and headlines splattered all over the news predict how the world is going to end. Stock markets crash and we head for a recession – a contraction or recession is associated with declines in most sectors, with inflation decreasing. When the recession reaches its trough, the economy brings a new expansion (recovery), economic growth returns and eventually jobs become more available.

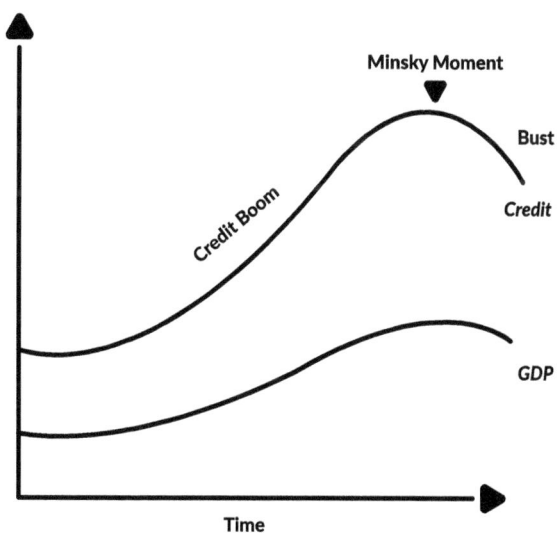

The tulip bubble

The tulip bubble of 1637 is probably the best example of a market crash. Tulip mania showed how a cultural trend and the madness of the crowd led to a catastrophic financial event.

A fashion for exotic tulips from Central Asia took hold of Dutch collectors in the mid-1600s, coincidentally at the same time that Dutch explorers discovered black swans in Australia. As demand increased, speculators began to stockpile seeds. Supplies became scarce, and the price of tulip bulbs increased rapidly – prices were going up twenty-fold each day. Everyone from farmers to noblemen believed that tulips were a good investment. Before long, people were trading their jewellery, life savings, land and personal belongings, and taking out loans in the belief that tulip bulbs would make them wealthier.

Options contracts were drawn – all of a sudden, people could pay a small premium (10%) to buy tulip bulbs at a fixed price. An option on a tulip bulb (currently worth 100 guilders) would cost the buyer only ten. If the price moved up to 200 guilders, the option holder would exercise their right, buying at 100 and simultaneously selling at 200.

Then, all of a sudden, a major player decided to get out of tulips and sold his entire load. There was nobody else in the market who could afford the bulbs. This, in turn, forced other sellers to lower the price. With an abundance of tulip supplies readily available, in no time at all, panic reigned in the streets of Amsterdam. Dealers went bankrupt and refused to honour their commitments. A government plan to settle all contracts at 10% of their face value was met with cynicism and frustration when the price of bulbs fell even lower. Before long, a tulip was cheaper than an onion in the vegetable market.[42]

Such rampant speculation still occurs today. Markets can be nearly impossible to predict in the short term. If someone is telling you what the next big thing is, they're either extremely dishonest or they don't know what they're talking about.

Over the course of history we have had several iterations of a tulip-style bubble: the South Sea Bubble, the Tech Wreck, the Great Depression and GFC are all examples of how markets are dictated by the extreme emotions of fear and greed. The moral of the story is that the herd will only pay for what is in demand.

The Kondratiev wave

People run from the market after a bubble bursts, but this too is an emotional reaction. In the long term, the

42 BG Malkiel, *A Random Walk Down Wall Street: The time-tested strategy for successful investing* (WW Norton & Company, New York, 2016), p38

market adjusts to the ripples of time and adapts, and smart investors can take advantage of this.

The Kondratiev wave, named after Russian economist Nikolai Kondratiev, is indicative of how markets and wealth pan out over the long term and explains the concept of large super cycles and normal business cycles. Kondratiev waves are long-term growth cycles that can range from forty to sixty years and consist of alternating intervals of high sectoral growth and relatively slow growth. These waves are driven by innovation.

Consider these examples.

- Industrial Revolution (1771)

- Age of steam and railways (1829)

- Age of steel and heavy engineering (1875)

- Age of oil, electricity, the automobile and mass production (1908)

- Age of information and telecommunications (1971)

- The 'gig' economy (2008–?)

The growth of long-term economic (business) cycles is attributed to demographic movements, inputs of labour and factors like the unemployment rate, workforce participation, aspiration of a society to do better, education, innovation in technology and human efforts, automation of capital replacing human labour and globalisation. The success and output of a country is referred to as gross domestic product (GDP), which is the total amount of income produced in that country. Changes in income on a GDP per-capita basis give an accurate reflection of success or failure. It is the rate of change in income and disposable income which largely reflects the confidence of people in a society.

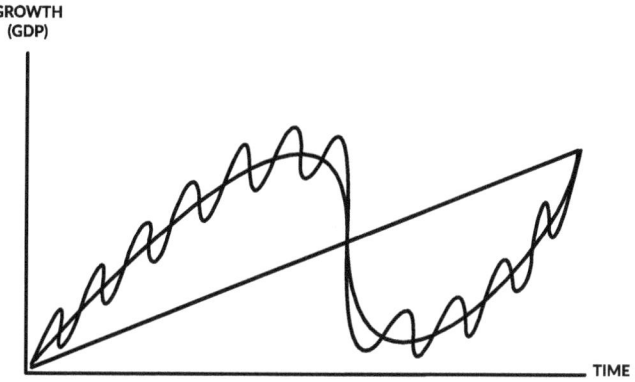

The human herd

Humans are mammals and move in a herd, but it is the herding of a crowd that leads to a bubble. Economics and finance are tricky beasts and it is important to know how they come together.

Markets are forward looking and the only thing they guarantee is innovation. The infallible law of demand is driven by the principle that resources are scarce, and it is fundamentally people's preferences that underpin the way that everything moves forward.

There will always be booms and busts which reoccur and repeat over time. As Sir Isaac Newton put it when commenting on the South Sea Bubble during his time as Master of the Mint: 'I can calculate the movement of the heavenly bodies but not the madness of people.'[43]

Money brings people together, because everyone wants money. For example, I can be an Australian backpacker travelling around Ecuador and understand the local merchant through the language of a US ten-dollar bill. And in its purest essence, money, whether it be tulips, silver or digits in a bank account, is a means of communication which circles throughout an economy. Our money is often a reflection of our values, preferences and undiluted emotions. For some, money is about achievement, freedom and adventure, while for others it's about security, integrity and providing for a family.

The wealth of a nation is indicative of income on a per-capita basis; there is a natural discourse where individual subjective values are translated into the objective information necessary for rational allocation of resources in society. What we can do is be conscious of our capitalist choices and make them about more than 'just' money, so every different coloured tulip

---

43 H Marks, *Mastering the Market Cycle: Getting the odds on your side* (Nicholas Brealey Publishing, Boston, 2018)

has an equal opportunity to have its time in the sun and bloom. The wellbeing of everyone depends on the cooperation and goodwill of the community.

Summary

Assets are classed according to their risks and rewards – the higher the risk, the greater the potential rewards, and potential losses. Each asset class, whether it's defensive assets like cash and bonds or growth assets like equities and property, has its own benefits and risks.

But beyond the cool consideration of risks and benefits, we must take our own human emotions into account. The key lesson here is to be aware of the madness of the crowd and remember to diversify not just across asset classes, but across markets. It is a matter of assessing all the risks and whether each is aligned to our goals; a thing is worth only what someone else will pay for it.

When it comes down to any investment, ask whether it is GREAT (see Chapter 1). Is taking on that amount of debt really worth your while? Or could you adjust the amount of risk that you are taking, maybe even reach your initial goal without the risks? Achieving a desired goal, eg to hit a certain income in retirement, grow your capital and reduce your tax, may require leverage, but you must still assess the risks and take financial theory into account.

For more information, check out the 'Investment Philosophy' in the resources section at www.equanimityfs.com.au/resources.

9
The Market

Markets are hard to predict in the short term. If you ask me what will happen next in the stock market, your guess is probably as good as mine – you could receive a huge range of returns depending on when you entered the market. Like any investment or starting a business, the first two years are usually the hardest. But in the long term, the law of averages applies and returns become stable and easy to determine.

In this chapter, I'll share my thoughts and insights on how I put together a portfolio for a client. We'll look at how the market is both rational and irrational, and the secret to optimising your strategy in the face of this: diversification. I'll introduce you to my 'three buckets' approach which will give you the best chance of managing your investments in the short, medium and long terms. Finally, we'll look at how markets all boil down to one thing: trust. And if you have trust in your own principles and get the right advice, you'll stay on track: the Tao of the market.

Predicting the market

Prospect theory

It is human nature to go for certainty over risk. In the 1970s, behavioural economists Daniel Kahneman and Amos Tversky developed an idea they called prospect theory.[44] As humans, we are naturally risk averse, and according to prospect theory we feel our losses twice as much as we feel our gains.

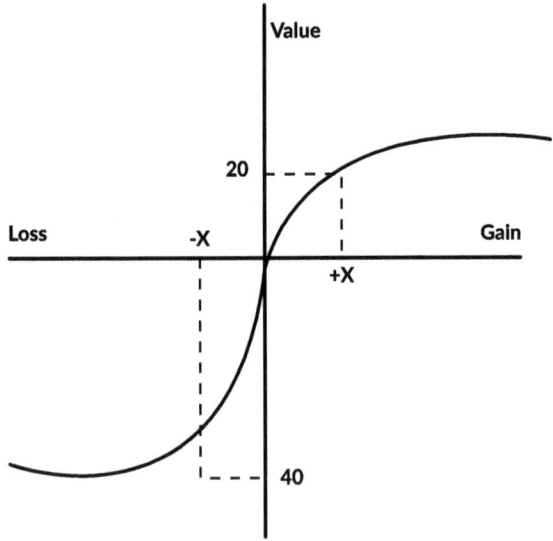

---

44   D Kahneman, *Thinking, Fast and Slow* (Farrar, Straus and Giroux, New York, 2011)

What prospect theory also takes into account is that as investors, we are not only risk averse, but we're prone to short-term biases such as overconfidence and mental accounting.

Rule of 72

But markets are actually quite predictable in the long term. The Rule of 72 is a quick, useful formula that is popularly used to estimate the number of years required to double the money you've invested at a given annual rate of return. While it is only an estimate, it gives you a representation of what to expect when you are investing and what your long-term future may look like when you're addressing the amount of risk you are willing to take and the reward you desire. This estimate, of course, doesn't take into account time and any black swan event.

The formula for the rule of 72 is:

$$\text{Years to double} = \frac{72}{\text{interest rate}}$$

Markets are near impossible to predict in the short term: nobody has a crystal ball to say when the next boom or bust is going to be. This begs the question – why do we forecast? As investment superstar Warren Buffett said, regarding the 'Noah principle', 'predicting rain doesn't count, building arcs does'.[45]

---

45 W Buffett, 'To the shareholders of Berkshire Hathaway Inc' [letter] (Berkshire Hathaway Inc, 1982), www.berkshirehathaway.com/ letters/1981.html, accessed 4 January 2021

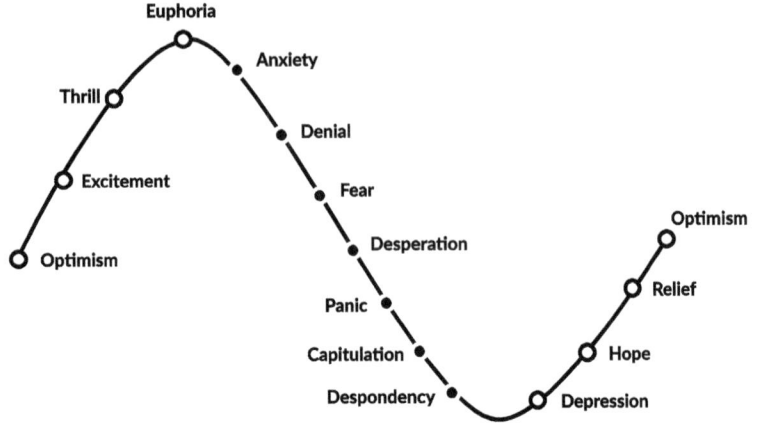

Are markets rational?

It sounds crazy, but markets are both rational and irrational at the same time. We've already seen how investing is an emotional (irrational) experience, but if everyone is constantly reacting to information from analysts and the dialogue between parties trading on an exchange, does that by its nature make markets rational? The answer – yes!

When it comes to markets, all information is considered public so is immediately 'priced' into a stock's value. While we can't as humans simply turn off our emotions, we can still analyse a company's balance sheet, earnings, cash flow and stewardship to maintain a competitive advantage within its industry. But there are times when information is limited and perhaps not always taken into consideration. Markets are generally neither perfectly efficient nor completely inefficient.

Market efficiency

The factors that affect a market's efficiency are:

- The number of participants (deep or shallow)

- Availability of information (information should not favour one person or another and should uphold the integrity of a market)

- Transaction and information costs

The only way to consider whether a market is fully efficient and information is immediately priced in is to analyse and determine a stock's intrinsic value. That is to say, ask what an analyst's opinion of a stock's value is based on its current financials (balance sheet) and future prospects (cash flows).

The secret of diversification

If markets are both rational and emotional at the same time, how do you ensure that your portfolios are optimised? The only way to protect yourself against the downside (systematic risk) and optimise the returns of a portfolio is to diversify. US economist Harry Markowitz found that a certain number of securities (shares in a company) across different industries reduced the risk of the portfolio.[46]

But it's not that simple. The graph below shows that increased diversification actually stops adding value. Over time, diversification becomes expensive, as an allocation of securities in a portfolio invested in a more concentrated fashion can increase the portfolio's returns.

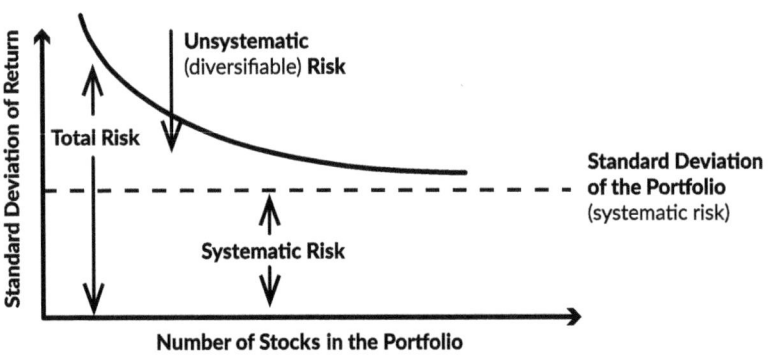

Three buckets

When you construct a portfolio, you need to examine whether it can be tailored to your individual circumstances. In most of the portfolios I put together, I adopt a core + satellite approach. This implies that we use simple financial instruments at a low cost (such as exchange traded funds) to form the 'heart' of

---

46   HM Markowitz, 'Portfolio selection', *The Journal of Finance*, 7:1 (March 1952), pp77–91

a portfolio's asset allocation, and a weighted portion of the portfolio designed to deliver value by creating outperformance or better returns on a 'risk-adjusted' basis (less risk but equal performance). Due to the unpredictability of markets and the subjectivity of investing, there's no golden principle, so I divide a portfolio into three 'buckets' which are aligned to a short-, medium- and long-term time horizon.

Your goals and agreed asset allocation will determine how many growth and defensive assets go into each of these buckets. A targeted asset allocation depends on several factors, such as the investor's risk tolerance, time horizon and investment objectives, and may change over time as circumstances change.

Bucket 1 – short term

Our first bucket is primarily there for a 'rainy day' and to take advantage of a bursting bubble. Cash is used in a portfolio to eliminate sequencing risk. Sequencing risk is where a negative return and withdrawals can have a significant impact on the long-term balance of your portfolio.

Consider the scenarios in Table 9.1. The first portfolio has a bad start with years that incur negative returns, while portfolio B starts positively.

Sequencing risk is the number-one concern when you're constructing a short-term portfolio. It is

Table 9.1: Sequencing risk

Year	Portfolio A	Returns	Portfolio B	Returns	Withdrawals	Difference
Initial Balance	$300,000		$300,000			
1	$258,750	-10%	$299,000	4%	$12,500	$40,250
2	$229,013	-7%	$349,530	22%	$12,500	$120,518
3	$238,164	10%	$353,882	5%	$12,500	$115,718
4	$214,381	-5%	$399,416	17%	$12,500	$185,036
5	$236,200	17%	$367,571	-5%	$12,500	$131,370
6	$212,515	-5%	$415,885	10%	$12,500	$203,370
7	$244,019	22%	$375,148	-7%	$12,500	$131,130
8	$222,258	-4%	$326,384	-10%	$12,500	$104,126

essential that there is a bucket of defensive assets or access to credit to inoculate yourself from a downturn and give you the ability to buy the dips.

What else goes into our first bucket? The first part of this bucket is having a portion invested as cash in a portfolio as a rainy-day fund to buy any dips, and/ or a particular style of investing known as dynamic investing. Dynamic asset allocation is a portfolio management strategy that frequently adjusts the mix of asset classes to suit market conditions. Adjustments usually involve reducing positions in the worst performing asset classes while adding to positions in the best performing assets.

Investments may sometimes be overpriced or underpriced, particularly over shorter timeframes, due to factors such as excessive investor optimism or fear as well as variations in market liquidity. In these situations, there is scope for a fund manager to add value or reduce risk by making timely adjustments to asset class allocations. Typically this would involve selling down assets they believe to be expensive or risky and increasing exposure to assets they deem to be cheap or of less risk.

A manager who has a dynamic asset allocation has a wide variance when it comes to investing and does not adhere to the traditional benchmarks. This style of investing can come in the form of a separately managed account or managed fund. A separately managed account is where the investor owns the underlying securities in their portfolio but allows a fund manager to make changes to the portfolio. A managed fund is an open-ended unit-trust structure, and the investor owns units in the fund as opposed to the underlying securities.

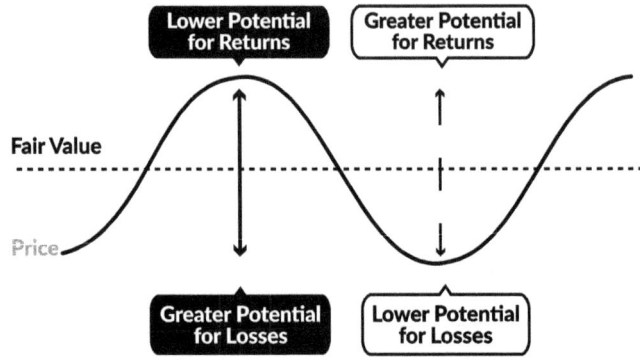

Over time, the intrinsic value of a security, whether equities or property, always reverts to the mean. Each investment has a firm anchor called intrinsic value. When prices fall below (or rise above) this intrinsic value, a buying (or selling) opportunity arises. It's the job of your financial advisor to reduce holdings of your assets that are demonstrating bubble-like tendencies.

Bucket 2 – medium term

The more you diversify, the costlier your investment becomes, and this actually diminishes its benefit. If you're already invested in the indexes of the ASX200 and S&P500, your investment has probably achieved enough diversification as it stands. The best processes adjust and prepare for all risks and make sure that the securities selected are adding value.

Whenever there is a macro-related trend (ie an oil shock or a boom in technology companies), there are stocks or particular asset classes that could stand to benefit from this trend, which could occur over a four-to-seven-year period. A manager of an actively managed fund will consider when to buy and, more importantly, when to get out of a particular stock. These types of fund managers aim to outperform a given benchmark – this is known as 'chasing alpha'.

It's important to ensure that active managers have some 'skin in the game' so it becomes a win-win where the fund manager or management firm puts investors first, and puts their own money where their mouth is. If a fund manager and their employees are putting their money in the fund, it signals to the market that they have conviction in what they're doing.

It's also important to consider the agency risk of a particular stock or bond – that is the ability for a company or bond issuer to deliver results – and compare it to its industry peers. When a fund loses conviction or isn't performing, it's removed from the portfolio.

Actively managed funds can be accessed via an investment wrap platform, usually charge a higher-than-normal fee and are designed to outperform an index. Depending on the fund, there can be a range of timeframes when your investment can be redeemed, usually ranging from three to ten business days from the time you decide to redeem the units invested.

Bucket 3 – long term

If a market is fully efficient, you can use a passive investment strategy by buying a broad market index, because active fund managers will underperform due to investment costs and management fees. A market index is a tool to track the performance of a group of securities listed on an exchange, such as the ASX200 (the top 200 companies listed on the Australian Stock Exchange) or S&P 500. There is a lot of evidence to suggest that in the long run, it is impossible to outperform an index.

This section of the portfolio is allocated to growth assets and requires an investment timeframe of at least seven years. The risk you need to address is longevity: you may outlive any of your savings and assets.

It's a good idea to use financial instruments called exchange-traded funds for the long-term bucket. These types of instruments merely track and follow the index (ASX200). Think of it as trying to find a needle in a haystack. Instead of buying individual securities (needle), you buy the whole haystack; that way, you diversify across everything. These types of instruments are listed on the ASX, are low cost and can be traded within Trade + two days.

The Tao of the market

The history of money can be traced back as far as 3000 BC to the civilisation of Sumer, where people were paid in units of barley. The Aztecs used the cocoa bean. Cigarettes have been used as currency in prisoner of war camps, and in Virginia, Maryland and North Carolina, tobacco was a currency up until the American Revolution. The reason these items worked as currency was because everyone understood their intrinsic value.

As societies have become more complicated and evolved, kingdoms and churches replaced finite goods with gold coins. Money is fiat (formally authorised); throughout time, it has been recognised as legal tender and a representation of a nation's sovereignty. A population's faith in the coin is a reflection of how much trust the people have in the monarch and respect for the nation's sovereignty at any given time.

In today's modern banking system, we operate in an ever more complicated and interconnected system of finance. Gone is the signature of the monarch, replaced with the digitisation of a nation's treasury. The currency you hold, noted as digits in your bank account, is a reflection of the trust you have in your country's banking system, and its guarantee by the government.

Central banks operate under instruction from governments, either printing money into circulation or retracting money by buying securities from subsidiary banks. They operate via a fractional banking system. Money flows away from banks, which must keep a minimum percentage of their holdings, usually 10%, but are free to loan out the other 90%.

Rational investors prefer to receive money today rather than the same amount in the future due to money's potential to grow in value over a given period of time. Our entire system of finance is dependent on people being able to access credit and repay loans. When we really think about it, money is a figment of our imaginations. How can a bank hold only 10% of its capital? Because we have invested our trust in it. The very success and failure of our society boils down to exactly that: an absence or presence of trust.

Markets are hugely complex systems that operate on trust, and to succeed in them, we must put our faith in their long-term stability. The Tao of the markets is found in keeping a cool head, rather than reacting with knee-jerk responses to the market. The single biggest mistake I see people make is letting their emotions get in the way and selling at the bottom of a market.

Such is the nature of humankind; markets are driven by extremes of fear and greed over a period. This herding behaviour results in bubbles. When markets are high, investors rush in with feelings of euphoria (greed). But what goes up must come back down as all bubbles eventually pop. Predictably, in times of despair, investors flee from markets and sell at the bottom of a crash, only to be re-inspired and invest at a later point in time.

Selling an investment at the bottom of the market and staying in cash even for a six-month period can have a significant impact on a portfolio's balance. As Benjamin Graham put it, 'The investor's chief problem, even his worst enemy, is likely to be himself'.[47]

---

47   B Graham, *The Intelligent Investor: A book of practical counsel* (Harper, New York, 1949)

Summary

Markets are emotional (irrational) and at the same time rational. In a similar way to the seasons, summer, autumn, winter and spring, we can rely on a continual cycle from boom to bust, and then a recovery.

We have seen how a strategy of three buckets can help to mitigate our risks when it comes to investing. While investing can be fun, there is always a risk. If you treat the stock market like a casino, it is likely to give you returns like a casino. By their very nature, markets are nearly impossible to predict in the short term, but in the long term, if you treat Mr Market with respect, he will give you respectful returns.

The essence of not trying to control your emotions is an emotional decision. Whether you're investing towards a goal or aiming to increase your total wealth, it is best to liaise with your trusted financial advisor to provide you with the right mentoring and insights so that you can enhance your wellbeing and livelihood. After all, there is a significant cost, one way or another, of getting it wrong should you do things yourself.

If you would like to know more, download a copy of the 'Value of Advice' brochure from the resources page at www.equanimityfs.com.au/resources.

Conclusion

You may think that you could never find peace fighting inside a cage, but that's what happened to me. My introduction to martial arts was through a twenty-two-week program that took twenty misfits, including myself, with zero talent or combat experience to a point where we could step inside a cage and compete against one another in an amateur mixed martial arts fight.

I am the biggest scaredy cat out there. I talk a brave game, but underneath it all, I'm a marshmallow. I detest violence and standing over someone is cowardly. But during that program, I was guided by some of the best coaches you could ask for – they are ambassadors for the community and teach self-respect and respect for others. They poured their energy and efforts into ensuring that every one of us was made to feel included, irrespective of gender or natural ability.

During the program, there were unbelievable transformations. Some people lost 20 kg, others who had been battling depression came through feeling great about themselves. On the night of the fight, introverts turned into gods, while those who were tipped to win learned to lose with grace.

I signed up to the program for purely selfish reasons: I had always wanted to learn a martial art, thinking that's what you do when you're a man. In my early twenties, I had contemplated joining the army just like my dad. He didn't have the best of childhoods and the army spring-boarded him to a successful career as a barrister. In turn, he had given me a prosperous and fortunate childhood, for which I am grateful. Perhaps there was a small part of me that wanted to get inside the ring to neutralise any of my own insecurities and prove to myself that I had the same convictions as my father.

On the first day of training, I struck up a conversation with another guy – let's call him Rick – of the same age, body type and ability as me, with perhaps a slightly more affable personality. We started training together and, throughout the twenty-two weeks, we maintained a close focus on one another's improvements. Both of us knew from the outset that come fight night, we could be matched against each another.

And that is what came to fruition – Rick and I locked horns in the second main event. He was the victor on the night, winning by a technical knockout. I took the loss with grace: the better man had won. We shook hands and shared a beer together with our friends and families, both sad to call an end on the whole experience.

After the program, each of us went our own way. Some of my fellow 'wimps' are now married with children; others have moved overseas. Rick moved back to Wales to be close to his family. As the months passed, we kept in sporadic contact via Facebook.

It was morning here when I woke up to Rick's comment in old Welsh slang: 'Keep yer old barny [head] up, mate,' to which I whimsically replied, 'Yeah right, mate, I'll make sure to slip slop slap [sun tan lotion] my bald boof-head, it's really hot over here.' At the time, I didn't understand the gravitas of his comment. Was it something much more profound? Two weeks later, I learned that Rick had decided to opt out of life on his own terms – he had passed.

I don't think I have ever been more scared in my life, hearing that someone who to me was the embodiment of fun could feel so helpless. I was mortified that such a wholesome, big-hearted person with so much potential had been tragically lost. Since then, I have never wanted anyone to feel as though they were alone.

As I get older, I realise that our career, money and wealth are just another means to an end. In the order and chaos of the world we live in, time is our most precious asset; it's the only thing we can never get back. While it's prudent to think about the future, one of the wisest things any of us can do is to appreciate the gift of the present and the power of the current moment.

The things that truly add value to our lives are not related to money. They are things like finding Zen; going about life with nothing to fear, nothing to prove, nothing to lose; forgiving; laughing often; treasuring friendships; and realising that in the light of every day's chaos, being grateful for what you have is an act of courage. It's amazing that a little bit of encouragement for another person can go a long way.

When it comes to building wealth, it is important to ask yourself who you are, not why you do things. Some of you reading this may be battling your own demons. They might be financial losses, but equally they might be emotional difficulties. Maybe your child is being bullied at school and you don't know what to do; maybe your job didn't go as planned; or maybe you stuffed up a relationship and it feels like the end of the world. But it's important to pull back and gain a broader perspective.

My Jiu-Jitsu coach puts things in perspective. One of the best things about learning a martial art like Brazilian Jiu-Jitsu is that it teaches us it is OK to lose. Understanding the need to experience and accept failure has been one of the most valuable lessons in my life. Learning to let go in the face of adversity is a powerful way to embrace the opportunity to grow. After all, setting a goal is like taking a step towards the person you would like to become. Whatever you choose to be, be a good one.

We stumble, accept that we made a mistake, and then we try again; there is no learning without loss. The difference between who you are and who you want to be lies in how you respond to difficulties and whether you choose to be positive. Welding yourself to a fixed outcome will never do you any favours; instead, decide that you will either win or learn.

If, through reading this book, you've gained a better understanding of how your finances can reflect your views and values, and you'd like to take the next step, there are several resources that can support you. Get a sense of how you are travelling in key areas of financial planning with the 'Equanimity Financial Services' scorecard that will give you a customised report and advice on where you can make improvements. Download yours from www.financialstrengthsscorecard. scoreapp.com. You can also download resources such as the detailed budget planner and white papers from www.equanimityfs.com.au / resources.

Acknowledgements

First of all, I would like to say a big thank you to you for reading this book. I am sure it will put a lot of things that are going on in your world into perspective.

A big thank you goes to Mum and Dad. You've given me the happiest of childhoods and your sacrifice has made me into the man that I am today. Also my younger brother, Jimmy, for your infectious personality, banter and always being there. To Nan and Pop – if somehow you manage to read this, we miss and love you both. Rest easy. To my mentor Neil (The Captain), thank you for being a great teacher. I couldn't have come this far without your guidance.

To all my mates, you're second to none. Never above, never below – always beside you.

The Author

Alex Galvin is the founder and principal advisor at Equanimity Financial Services. He takes the time to really understand what's important for his clients now and what they want to achieve both financially and personally.

Alex has worked for some of Australia's leading financial advice firms. He has achieved a Certified Financial Planning designation, the highest award in the industry, and has a Bachelor's degree in Commerce-Marketing, a Master's in Financial Planning and is licensed to provide advice on self-managed superannuation funds.

In his spare time, you'll find him surfing, training in Brazilian Jiu-Jitsu and enjoying a pale ale (maybe even a chardonnay) with friends and family on Manly beach.

Contact

Alex would love to connect with you on social media – look him up online at:

🌐 www.equanimityfs.com.au

💼 @alexgalvinefs

📘 @Equanimityfs

📷 @equanimity_fs

Lightning Source UK Ltd.
Milton Keynes UK
UKHW021826090321
380064UK00006B/251